Instant Pot® COOKBOOK

GOOD FOOD *FAST!*

Publications International, Ltd.

Pictured on the front cover *(clockwise from top left):* Garlic Parmesan Spaghetti Squash
(page 133), Salsa Verde Chicken Stew *(page 37)* and Italian Beef Sandwiches *(page 70).*

Pictured on the back cover *(clockwise from top left):* Sweet Potato and Black Bean Chili
(page 54), Easy Meatballs *(page 102),* Perfect BBQ Ribs *(page 83)* and Tuesday Night Tacos
(page 80).

ISBN: 978-1-63938-389-4

Manufactured in China.

8 7 6 5 4 3 2 1

Let's get social!

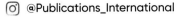

○ @Publications_International

f @PublicationsInternational

www.pilbooks.com

CONTENTS

Instant Pot

GOOD FOOD MADE FAST

Preparing one, two or three meals a day can be exhausting, so let your Instant Pot—and the magic of pressure cooking—do the work for you. The recipes in this book were designed to minimize the time and energy you spend on cooking, with fewer steps and less cooking time than conventional recipes. But your family can still enjoy all their favorites, from mac and cheese and meatballs to chicken soup and chili—they'll just be quicker and easier to make than they used to be.

WHY USE A PRESSURE COOKER?

Speed is the main reason. In pressure cooking, liquid is heated in a heavy pot with a lid that locks and forms an airtight seal. Since the steam from the hot liquid is trapped inside and can't evaporate, the pressure increases and raises the boiling point of the contents in the pot, and these items cook faster at a higher temperature. In general, pressure cooking can reduce cooking time to about one third of the time used in conventional cooking methods—and typically the time spent on pressure cooking is hands off. (There's no peeking or stirring when food is being cooked under pressure.)

WHAT MAKES THE INSTANT POT DIFFERENT?

The Instant Pot is a versatile electric multi-cooker that can be a pressure cooker, rice cooker, slow cooker, steamer and yogurt maker. The cooking programs you'll find on the control panel are convenient shortcuts for some foods you may prepare regularly (rice, beans, etc.) which use preset times and cooking levels. But in these pages we'll explore the basics of pressure cooking with recipes that use the Pressure Cook or Manual button along with customized cooking times and pressure levels. These simple and delicious dishes will inspire you to use your Instant Pot daily and create your own Instant Pot magic!

Butter Chicken *(page 90)*

Mu Shu Turkey *(page 68)*

Orecchiette with Sausage and Broccoli Rabe *(page 118)*

INSTANT POT COMPONENTS

The **exterior pot** is where the electrical components are housed. It should never be immersed in water; to clean it, simply unplug the unit, wipe it with a damp cloth and dry it immediately.

The **inner pot** holds the food and fits snugly into the exterior pot. Made of stainless steel, it is removable, and it can be washed by hand or in the dishwasher.

The **LED display** shows a time that indicates where the pressure cooker is in a particular function. The time counts down to zero from the number of minutes that were programmed. (The timing begins once the machine reaches pressure.) For Keep Warm and Yogurt functions, the time counts up.

The **pressure release valve** is on top of the lid and is used to seal the pot or release steam. To seal the pot, move the valve to the Sealing position; to release pressure, move the valve to the Venting position. This valve can pop off to clean, and to make sure nothing is blocking it.

The **float valve** controls the amount of pressure inside the pressure cooker and indicates when pressure cooking is taking place. The valve rises once the contents of the pot reach working pressure; it drops down when all the pressure has been released after cooking.

The **anti-block shield** is a small stainless steel cage found on the inside of the lid that prevents the pressure cooker from clogging. It can be removed for cleaning.

The **silicone sealing ring** underneath the lid helps create a tight seal to facilitate pressure cooking. The sealing ring has a tendency to absorb strong odors from cooking (particularly from acidic ingredients); washing it regularly with warm soapy water or in the dishwasher will help these odors dissipate, as will storing your Instant Pot with the lid ring side up. If you cook both sweet and savory dishes frequently, you may want to purchase an extra sealing ring (so the scent of curry or pot roast doesn't affect your rice pudding or crème brûlée). Make sure to inspect the ring before cooking—if it has any splits or cracks, it will not work properly and should be replaced.

INSTANT POT COOKING BASICS

Every recipe is slightly different, but most include these basic steps. Read through the entire recipe before beginning to cook so you'll know what ingredients to add and when to add them, which pressure level to use, the cooking time and the release method.

1. Sauté: Many recipes call for sautéing vegetables or browning meat at the beginning of a recipe to add flavor. (Be sure to leave the lid off in this step.)

2. Add the ingredients as the recipe directs and secure the lid, making sure the arrow mark on the lid is aligned with the "close" mark and lock icon on the rim of the outside pot. Turn the pressure release valve to the Sealing position.

3. Select Pressure Cook or Manual, then choose the pressure level. The default setting is high pressure, which is what most recipes in this book use. To change to low pressure, use the Pressure Level or Adjust button. To set the cooking time, use the + and - buttons. The Instant Pot will start automatically.

4. Once the pressure cooking is complete, use the pressure release method directed by the recipe. There are three types of releases:

Natural release:

Let the pressure slowly release on its own, which can take anywhere from 5 to 25 minutes (but is typically in the 10- to 15-minute range). The release time will be shorter for a pot that is less full and longer for one that is more full. When the float valve lowers, the pressure is released and you can open the lid.

Quick release:

Use a towel or pot holder to manually turn the pressure valve to the Venting position immediately after the cooking is complete. (Be sure to get out of the way of the steam before turning the valve.) It can take up to 2 minutes to fully release all the pressure; the float valve will drop down when all the pressure is released.

A combination of natural and quick release:

The recipe will instruct you to let the pressure release naturally for a certain amount of time (frequently for 10 minutes), and then do a quick release as directed.

TIPS, TRICKS, DOS AND DON'TS

- Read the manual before beginning. There may be features you won't use, but it will eliminate some beginner's confusion, and it can help you understand how the Instant Pot works—and see all its possibilities. Models also change over time, so the manual can provide the best information about the buttons and functions of your pot. (Note that the terms "Pressure Cook" and "Manual" are interchangeable.)

- Don't overfill the pot—the total amount of food and liquid should not exceed the maximum level marked on the inner pot. Generally it is best not to fill the pot more than two thirds full; when cooking foods that expand during cooking such as beans and grains, do not fill it more than half full.

- Make sure there is always some liquid in the pot before cooking because a minimum amount is required to come up to pressure (the amount differs between models). However, if the recipe contains a large quantity of vegetables or meats, you may be able to use a bit less since these ingredients will create their own liquid.

- Always check that the pressure release valve is in the right position before you start pressure cooking. The food simply won't get cooked if the valve is not in the Sealing position because there will not be enough pressure in the pot.

- Never try to force the lid open after cooking—if the lid won't open, that means the pressure has not fully released. (As a safety feature, the lid remains locked until the float valve drops down.)

- Save the thickeners for after the pressure cooking is done. Pressure cooker recipes often end up with a lot of flavorful liquid left in the pot when cooking is complete; flour or cornstarch mixtures can thicken these liquids into delicious sauces. Use the Sauté function while incorporating the thickeners into the cooking liquid, and then cook and stir until the desired consistency is reached.

- Keep in mind that cooking times in some recipes may vary. We've included pressure cooking time charts as a guide (pages 184–187), but these are approximate times, and numerous variables may cause your results to be different. For example, the freshness of dried beans affects their cooking time (older beans take longer to cook), as does what they are cooked with—hard water (water that is high in mineral content), acidic ingredients, sugar and salt levels can also affect cooking times. So be flexible and experiment with what works best for you—you can always check the doneness of your food and add more time.

- Set reasonable expectations, i.e., don't expect everything you cook in the Instant Pot to be ready in a few minutes. Even though it reduces many conventional cooking times dramatically, nothing is literally "instant"—it will always take time to get up to pressure, and then to release it. (These machines are fast but not magical!)

Instant Pot®

SOUPS

COCONUT CURRY CHICKEN SOUP
MAKES 4 SERVINGS

1 can (about 13 ounces) coconut milk, divided

1½ cups chicken broth

1 cup chopped onion

2 tablespoons curry powder

1 teaspoon salt

½ teaspoon ground ginger

⅛ teaspoon ground red pepper

1½ pounds boneless skinless chicken thighs

¼ cup chopped fresh cilantro or mint

2 cups cooked rice (optional)

Lime wedges (optional)

1 Shake or stir coconut milk until well blended and smooth. Combine half of coconut milk, broth, onion, curry powder, salt, ginger and red pepper in Instant Pot; mix well. Add chicken, pressing into liquid.

2 Secure lid and move pressure release valve to Sealing position. Press Pressure Cook or Manual; cook at high pressure 9 minutes.

3 When cooking is complete, use natural release for 10 minutes, then release remaining pressure. Remove chicken to plate; let stand until cool enough to handle.

4 Shred chicken into bite-size pieces. Press Sauté; add chicken to pot with remaining coconut milk and cilantro. Cook 3 minutes or until heated through, stirring occasionally. Spoon rice over each serving, if desired; serve with lime wedges.

MUSHROOM BARLEY SOUP
MAKES 6 TO 8 SERVINGS

2 tablespoons olive oil

1 onion, chopped

2 carrots, chopped

2 stalks celery, chopped

3 cloves garlic, minced

1 teaspoon salt

½ teaspoon dried thyme

½ teaspoon black pepper

5 cups vegetable or chicken broth

1 package (16 ounces) sliced mushrooms

½ cup uncooked pearl barley

½ ounce dried porcini or shiitake mushrooms

1 Press Sauté; heat oil in Instant Pot. Add onion, carrots and celery; cook and stir 5 minutes or until vegetables are softened. Add garlic, salt, thyme and pepper; cook and stir 1 minute. Stir in broth, sliced mushrooms, barley and dried mushrooms; mix well.

2 Secure lid and move pressure release valve to Sealing position. Press Pressure Cook or Manual; cook at high pressure 22 minutes.

3 When cooking is complete, use natural release for 10 minutes, then release remaining pressure.

CHICKEN TORTILLA SOUP
MAKES 4 TO 6 SERVINGS

2 cans (about 14 ounces each) diced tomatoes

1½ pounds boneless skinless chicken thighs

1 onion, chopped

½ cup chicken broth

1 can (4 ounces) diced green chiles

2 cloves garlic, minced

1 teaspoon salt

1 teaspoon ground cumin

¼ teaspoon black pepper

4 corn tortillas, cut into ¼-inch strips

2 tablespoons chopped fresh cilantro

½ cup (2 ounces) shredded Monterey Jack cheese

1 avocado, diced and tossed with lime juice

Lime wedges

1 Combine tomatoes, chicken, onion, broth, chiles, garlic, salt, cumin and pepper in Instant Pot; mix well.

2 Secure lid and move pressure release valve to Sealing position. Press Pressure Cook or Manual; cook at high pressure 9 minutes.

3 When cooking is complete, use natural release for 10 minutes, then release remaining pressure.

4 Remove chicken to plate; let stand until cool enough to handle. Shred chicken into bite-size pieces; stir into soup.

5 Press Sauté; add tortillas and cilantro to soup. Cook and stir 2 minutes or until heated through. Top with cheese, avocado and squeeze of lime juice. Serve immediately.*

If desired, soup can be made ahead through step 4. When ready to serve, heat soup to a simmer; add tortilla strips and cilantro and cook until heated through.

SPLIT PEA SOUP
MAKES 4 TO 6 SERVINGS

8 slices bacon, chopped

1 onion, chopped

2 carrots, chopped

1 stalk celery, chopped

1 clove garlic, minced

½ teaspoon dried thyme

4 cups chicken broth

2 cups water

1 package (16 ounces) dried split peas, rinsed and sorted

¾ teaspoon salt

½ teaspoon black pepper

1 bay leaf

1 Press Sauté; cook bacon in Instant Pot until crisp. Remove to paper towel-lined plate. Drain off all but 1 tablespoon drippings.

2 Add onion, carrots and celery to pot; cook and stir 5 minutes or until vegetables are softened. Add garlic and thyme; cook and stir 1 minute. Stir in broth and water, scraping up browned bits from bottom of pot. Add split peas, half of bacon, salt, pepper and bay leaf; mix well.

3 Secure lid and move pressure release valve to Sealing position. Press Pressure Cook or Manual; cook at high pressure 8 minutes.

4 When cooking is complete, use natural release for 10 minutes, then release remaining pressure. Stir soup; remove and discard bay leaf. Garnish with remaining bacon.

NOTE

The soup may seem thin immediately after cooking, but it will thicken upon standing. If prepared in advance and refrigerated, thin the soup with water when reheating until it reaches the desired consistency.

NORTH AFRICAN CHICKEN SOUP
MAKES 4 TO 6 SERVINGS

1 tablespoon vegetable oil

1 cup chopped onion

3 cloves garlic, minced

¾ teaspoon paprika

½ teaspoon ground ginger

½ teaspoon ground cumin

¼ teaspoon ground allspice

1¼ pounds sweet potatoes, peeled and cut into 1-inch pieces (2½ cups)

2 cups chicken broth

1 can (about 14 ounces) whole tomatoes, undrained, cut up or crushed with hands

12 ounces boneless skinless chicken thighs, cut into 1-inch pieces

½ teaspoon salt

¼ to ½ teaspoon black pepper

Hot pepper sauce and lime juice (optional)

1 Press Sauté; heat oil in Instant Pot. Add onion; cook and stir 3 minutes or until softened. Add garlic; cook and stir 30 seconds. Add paprika, ginger, cumin and allspice; cook and stir 30 seconds. Stir in sweet potatoes, broth, tomatoes with juice, chicken and salt; mix well.

2 Secure lid and move pressure release valve to Sealing position. Press Pressure Cook or Manual; cook at high pressure 5 minutes.

3 When cooking is complete, use natural release for 10 minutes, then release remaining pressure. Stir in black pepper to taste. Serve with hot pepper sauce and lime juice, if desired.

LENTIL RICE SOUP
MAKES 4 TO 6 SERVINGS

1 tablespoon olive oil

1 onion, finely chopped

2 carrots, finely chopped

2 stalks celery, finely chopped

2 teaspoons minced garlic

1 teaspoon salt

1 teaspoon herbes de Provence

⅛ teaspoon black pepper

6 cups vegetable broth

1 cup dried lentils, rinsed and sorted

¼ cup uncooked rice, rinsed well and drained

¼ cup chopped fresh parsley

Sour cream (optional)

1 Press Sauté; heat oil in Instant Pot. Add onion, carrots, celery and garlic; cook and stir 5 minutes or until vegetables are softened. Add salt, herbes de Provence and pepper; cook and stir 30 seconds. Stir in broth, lentils and rice; mix well.

2 Secure lid and move pressure release valve to Sealing position. Press Pressure Cook or Manual; cook at high pressure 10 minutes.

3 When cooking is complete, use natural release for 10 minutes, then release remaining pressure. Stir in parsley. Top with sour cream, if desired.

POZOLE
MAKES 4 TO 6 SERVINGS

1 tablespoon olive oil

1 large onion, cut in half and cut into ¼-inch slices

2 teaspoons dried oregano

1 clove garlic, minced

½ teaspoon ground cumin

3 cups chicken broth

12 ounces boneless skinless chicken thighs, cut into 1-inch strips

2 cans (4 ounces each) diced green chiles

¼ teaspoon salt

1 package (10 ounces) frozen corn

1 can (2¼ ounces) sliced black olives, drained

Chopped fresh cilantro (optional)

Lime wedges (optional)

1 Press Sauté; heat oil in Instant Pot. Add onion; cook and stir 3 minutes or until softened. Add oregano, garlic and cumin; cook and stir 1 minute. Stir in broth, chicken, chiles and salt; mix well.

2 Secure lid and move pressure release valve to Sealing position. Press Pressure Cook or Manual; cook at high pressure 5 minutes.

3 When cooking is complete, use natural release for 10 minutes, then release remaining pressure.

4 Press Sauté; add corn and olives to soup. Cook and stir 3 minutes or until heated through. Garnish with cilantro; serve with lime wedges, if desired.

BEEF FAJITA SOUP
MAKES 8 SERVINGS

1 pound beef stew meat (1-inch pieces)

1 can (about 15 ounces) pinto beans, rinsed and drained

1 can (about 15 ounces) black beans, rinsed and drained

1 can (about 14 ounces) beef broth

1 can (about 10 ounces) diced tomatoes with green chiles

1 green bell pepper, cut into ½-inch slices

1 red bell pepper, cut into ½-inch slices

1 onion, cut into ¼-inch slices

2 teaspoons ground cumin

1 teaspoon seasoned salt

½ teaspoon black pepper

Optional toppings: sour cream, shredded Monterey Jack or Cheddar cheese, chopped olives

1 Combine beef, beans, broth, tomatoes, bell peppers, onion, cumin, seasoned salt and black pepper in Instant Pot; mix well.

2 Secure lid and move pressure release valve to Sealing position. Press Pressure Cook or Manual; cook at high pressure 25 minutes.

3 When cooking is complete, use natural release for 10 minutes, then release remaining pressure. Serve with desired toppings.

CHICKEN ORZO SOUP
MAKES 6 TO 8 SERVINGS

1 tablespoon vegetable oil

1 onion, chopped

1 bulb fennel, quartered, cored and thinly sliced (reserve fronds for garnish)

2 teaspoons minced garlic

6 cups chicken broth

1½ pounds boneless skinless chicken breasts

2 carrots, peeled and cut into ¼-inch slices

2 sprigs fresh thyme

1 bay leaf

¾ teaspoon salt

¼ teaspoon black pepper

½ cup uncooked orzo

1 Press Sauté; heat oil in Instant Pot. Add onion and fennel; cook and stir about 6 minutes or until tender. Add garlic; cook and stir 1 minute. Stir in broth, chicken, carrots, thyme, bay leaf, salt and pepper; mix well.

2 Secure lid and move pressure release valve to Sealing position. Press Pressure Cook or Manual; cook at high pressure 9 minutes.

3 When cooking is complete, use natural release for 10 minutes, then release remaining pressure. Remove chicken to plate; let stand until cool enough to handle.

4 Meanwhile, press Sauté; add orzo to pot. Cook about 10 minutes or until orzo is tender, stirring occasionally. Remove and discard thyme sprigs and bay leaf.

5 Shred chicken into bite-size pieces. Return chicken to pot; mix well. Garnish soup with fennel fronds.

CREAMY TOMATO SOUP
MAKES 6 SERVINGS

2 tablespoons olive oil

2 tablespoons butter

1 large onion, finely chopped

2 cloves garlic, minced

2 teaspoons sugar

1½ teaspoons salt

½ teaspoon dried oregano

2 cans (28 ounces each) peeled Italian plum tomatoes, undrained

Focaccia Croutons (recipe follows, optional)

½ cup whipping cream

1 Press Sauté; heat oil and butter in Instant Pot. Add onion; cook and stir 5 minutes or until softened. Add garlic, sugar, salt and oregano; cook and stir 30 seconds. Stir in tomatoes with juice; mix well.

2 Secure lid and move pressure release valve to Sealing position. Press Pressure Cook or Manual; cook at high pressure 8 minutes. Prepare Focaccia Croutons, if desired.

3 When cooking is complete, use natural release for 10 minutes, then release remaining pressure.

4 Use hand-held immersion blender to blend soup until smooth. Stir in cream until well blended. Serve soup with croutons.

FOCACCIA CROUTONS

Combine 4 cups ½-inch focaccia cubes (half of 9-ounce loaf), 1 tablespoon olive oil and ½ teaspoon black pepper in large bowl; toss to coat. Spread on large baking sheet; bake in preheated 350°F oven about 10 minutes or until golden brown.

PORK AND CABBAGE SOUP
MAKES 6 SERVINGS

8 ounces pork loin, cut into ½-inch pieces

1 medium onion, chopped

2 slices bacon, finely chopped

1 can (about 28 ounces) whole tomatoes, undrained, coarsely chopped

1 teaspoon salt

1 bay leaf

¾ teaspoon dried marjoram

⅛ teaspoon black pepper

½ medium green cabbage, chopped, divided (about 5 cups)

2 medium carrots, cut into ½-inch slices

1 cup chicken broth

2 tablespoons chopped fresh parsley

1 Press Sauté; add pork, onion and bacon to Instant Pot. Cook and stir about 5 minutes or until pork is no longer pink and onion is softened. Add tomatoes with juice, salt, bay leaf, marjoram and pepper; cook 2 minutes, scraping up browned bits from bottom of pot. Stir in half of cabbage, carrots and broth; mix well.

2 Secure lid and move pressure release valve to Sealing position. Press Pressure Cook or Manual; cook at high pressure 8 minutes.

3 When cooking is complete, use natural release for 10 minutes, then release remaining pressure. Remove and discard bay leaf.

4 Press Sauté; add remaining half of cabbage to pot. Cook about 3 minutes or until cabbage is wilted, stirring frequently. Stir in parsley.

ONE-POT CHINESE CHICKEN SOUP
MAKES 4 SERVINGS

4 cups chicken broth

⅓ cup reduced-sodium
    soy sauce

1 pound boneless skinless
    chicken thighs

1 package (16 ounces)
    frozen stir-fry
    vegetables
    (do not thaw)

6 ounces uncooked thin
    Chinese egg noodles

1 to 3 tablespoons
    sriracha sauce

1 Combine broth and soy sauce in Instant Pot; mix well. Add chicken. Secure lid and move pressure release valve to Sealing position. Press Pressure Cook or Manual; cook at high pressure 8 minutes.

2 When cooking is complete, use quick release. Remove chicken to plate; let stand 5 minutes or until cool enough to handle. Shred chicken into bite-size pieces.

3 Press Sauté; add vegetables and noodles to broth mixture in pot. Cook about 3 minutes or until noodles are tender.

4 Stir in chicken and 1 tablespoon sriracha sauce; taste and add additional sauce for a spicier flavor.

WEST AFRICAN PEANUT SOUP
MAKES 6 TO 8 SERVINGS

2 tablespoons vegetable oil

1 large onion, chopped

½ cup chopped roasted peanuts

1½ tablespoons minced fresh ginger

4 cloves garlic, minced (about 1 tablespoon)

1 teaspoon salt

3 cups vegetable broth

⅓ cup unsweetened peanut butter (creamy or chunky)

2 sweet potatoes, peeled and cut into ½-inch cubes

1 can (28 ounces) whole tomatoes, drained and coarsely chopped

1 bunch kale or Swiss chard, stemmed and shredded

¼ teaspoon ground red pepper

1 Press Sauté; heat oil in Instant Pot. Add onion; cook and stir 5 minutes or until softened. Add peanuts, ginger, garlic and salt; cook and stir 1 minute.

2 Stir in broth and peanut butter until blended. Add sweet potatoes, tomatoes, kale and red pepper; mix well.

3 Secure lid and move pressure release valve to Sealing position. Press Pressure Cook or Manual; cook at high pressure 3 minutes.

4 When cooking is complete, use quick release.

Instant Pot®

STEWS & CHILIES

SALSA VERDE CHICKEN STEW
MAKES 4 TO 6 SERVINGS

2 cans (about 15 ounces each) black beans, rinsed and drained

1½ pounds boneless skinless chicken breasts, cut into 1-inch pieces

1 jar (16 ounces) salsa verde

1½ cups frozen corn

¾ cup chopped fresh cilantro

Diced avocado (optional)

1 Combine beans, chicken and salsa in Instant Pot; mix well.

2 Secure lid and move pressure release valve to Sealing position. Press Pressure Cook or Manual; cook at high pressure 4 minutes.

3 When cooking is complete, use quick release.

4 Press Sauté; add corn to pot. Cook about 3 minutes or until heated through. Stir in cilantro; mix well. Garnish with avocado.

CORN AND SWEET POTATO CURRY
MAKES 6 SERVINGS

1 tablespoon vegetable oil

1 large onion, chopped

2 tablespoons minced fresh ginger

½ jalapeño pepper, seeded and minced

2 cloves garlic, minced

1 cup frozen corn

2 teaspoons curry powder

½ teaspoon salt

1 can (about 13 ounces) coconut milk, well shaken

1 tablespoon soy sauce

4 sweet potatoes, peeled and cut into ¾-inch cubes

Hot cooked jasmine or long grain rice

Optional toppings: chopped fresh cilantro, finely chopped green onions, chopped roasted peanuts

1 Press Sauté; heat oil in Instant Pot. Add onion, ginger, jalapeño and garlic; cook and stir 3 minutes or until softened. Add corn, curry powder and salt; cook and stir 1 minute. Add coconut milk and soy sauce; stir until well blended. Stir in sweet potatoes; mix well.

2 Secure lid and move pressure release valve to Sealing position. Press Pressure Cook or Manual; cook at high pressure 3 minutes.

3 When cooking is complete, use quick release.

4 Press Sauté; cook about 2 minutes or until stew is thickened to desired consistency. Serve over rice; garnish as desired.

BLACK AND WHITE CHILI
MAKES 4 SERVINGS

1 tablespoon vegetable oil

1 pound chicken tenders, cut into ¾-inch pieces

1 cup coarsely chopped onion

1 can (about 14 ounces) fire-roasted diced tomatoes

1 can (about 15 ounces) Great Northern beans, rinsed and drained

1 can (about 15 ounces) black beans, rinsed and drained

2 tablespoons chili seasoning mix

¾ teaspoon salt

Hot pepper sauce (optional)

1 Press Sauté; heat oil in Instant Pot. Add chicken and onion; cook and stir 5 minutes or until chicken begins to brown. Add tomatoes; cook 1 minute, scraping up browned bits from bottom of pot. Stir in beans, chili seasoning mix and salt; mix well.

2 Secure lid and move pressure release valve to Sealing position. Press Pressure Cook or Manual; cook at high pressure 5 minutes.

3 When cooking is complete, use natural release for 10 minutes, then release remaining pressure. Serve with hot pepper sauce, if desired.

CURRIED CHICKEN AND WINTER VEGETABLE STEW
MAKES 4 TO 6 SERVINGS

1 tablespoon vegetable oil

1 medium onion, chopped

1 tablespoon curry powder

1 clove garlic, minced

1 pound boneless skinless chicken breasts, cut into ½-inch pieces

1 can (about 14 ounces) diced tomatoes

1 cup chicken broth

2 medium turnips, cut into 1-inch pieces

2 medium carrots, cut into 1-inch slices

½ cup raisins (optional)

¼ cup tomato paste

1 teaspoon salt

⅛ teaspoon ground red pepper

1 Press Sauté; heat oil in Instant Pot. Add onion; cook and stir 3 minutes or until softened. Add curry powder and garlic; cook and stir 1 minute. Stir in chicken, tomatoes, broth, turnips, carrots, raisins, if desired, tomato paste, salt and red pepper; mix well.

2 Secure lid and move pressure release valve to Sealing position. Press Pressure Cook or Manual; cook at high pressure 5 minutes.

3 When cooking is complete, use natural release for 5 minutes, then release remaining pressure.

SERVING SUGGESTION
Serve with couscous or brown rice.

THREE BEAN TURKEY CHILI
MAKES 8 SERVINGS

1 tablespoon olive oil

1 pound ground turkey

1 medium onion, chopped

2 tablespoons chili powder

1½ teaspoons smoked paprika

1½ teaspoons ground cumin

1 can (28 ounces)
   diced tomatoes

1 can (about 15 ounces)
   chickpeas, rinsed
   and drained

1 can (about 15 ounces)
   kidney beans, rinsed
   and drained

1 can (about 15 ounces)
   black beans, rinsed
   and drained

1 can (6 ounces) tomato
   sauce

1 can (4 ounces) diced
   green chiles

⅓ cup chicken broth or water

1½ teaspoons salt

1 Press Sauté; heat oil in Instant Pot. Add turkey and onion; cook about 6 minutes or until turkey is no longer pink and onion is softened, stirring to break up meat. Add chili powder, paprika and cumin; cook and stir 2 minutes. Stir in tomatoes, chickpeas, beans, tomato sauce, chiles, broth and salt; mix well.

2 Secure lid and move pressure release valve to Sealing position. Press Pressure Cook or Manual; cook at high pressure 15 minutes.

3 When cooking is complete, use natural release for 10 minutes, then release remaining pressure. If there is excess liquid, press Sauté and cook 5 minutes or until thickened.

SAVORY COD STEW
MAKES 6 TO 8 SERVINGS

8 ounces bacon, chopped

1 large onion, diced

1 large carrot, diced

2 stalks celery, diced

2 cloves garlic, minced

1 can (28 ounces) plum tomatoes, undrained, coarsely chopped

2 potatoes, peeled and diced

1 cup clam juice

3 tablespoons tomato paste

3 tablespoons chopped fresh Italian parsley

½ teaspoon salt

¼ teaspoon black pepper

3 saffron threads

2½ pounds fresh cod, skin removed, cut into 1½-inch pieces

1 Press Sauté; cook bacon in Instant Pot until crisp. Drain off all but 2 tablespoons drippings.

2 Add onion, carrot, celery and garlic to pot; cook and stir 5 minutes or until vegetables are softened. Add tomatoes with juice, potatoes, clam juice, tomato paste, parsley, salt, pepper and saffron; cook and stir 2 minutes.

3 Secure lid and move pressure release valve to Sealing position. Press Pressure Cook or Manual; cook at high pressure 2 minutes.

4 When cooking is complete, use quick release. Add cod to pot. Secure lid and move pressure release valve to Sealing position. Press Pressure Cook or Manual; cook at low pressure 1 minute.

5 When cooking is complete, use quick release.

CHICKEN ENCHILADA CHILI
MAKES 4 SERVINGS

1 can (about 14 ounces) diced tomatoes with green chiles

1 can (10 ounces) red enchilada sauce

½ teaspoon salt

¼ teaspoon ground cumin

⅛ teaspoon black pepper

1½ pounds boneless skinless chicken thighs, cut into 1-inch pieces

1 cup frozen or canned corn

1½ tablespoons cornmeal

2 tablespoons finely chopped fresh cilantro

½ cup (2 ounces) shredded pepper jack cheese

Sliced green onions (optional)

1 Combine tomatoes, enchilada sauce, salt, cumin and pepper in Instant Pot; mix well. Add chicken; stir to coat.

2 Secure lid and move pressure release valve to Sealing position. Press Pressure Cook or Manual; cook at high pressure 5 minutes.

3 When cooking is complete, use natural release for 10 minutes, then release remaining pressure.

4 Press Sauté; add corn and cornmeal to pot. Cook about 6 minutes or until chili thickens, stirring frequently. Stir in cilantro. Sprinkle with cheese; garnish with green onions.

GREEN CURRY WITH TOFU
MAKES 2 TO 4 SERVINGS

1 tablespoon vegetable oil

1 onion, chopped

⅓ cup Thai green curry paste

1 can (about 13 ounces) coconut milk, well shaken

1 package (14 ounces) firm tofu, drained and cut into 1-inch cubes

1 cup cut green beans (1-inch pieces)

1 broccoli crown (about 8 ounces), cut into florets

2 teaspoons water

1 teaspoon cornstarch

½ teaspoon salt

Hot cooked brown rice or rice noodles

1 Press Sauté; heat oil in Instant Pot. Add onion; cook and stir 5 minutes or until onion is soft and lightly browned. Add curry paste and coconut milk; mix well. Add tofu, green beans and broccoli. (Do not stir.)

2 Secure lid and move pressure release valve to Sealing position. Press Pressure Cook or Manual; cook at high pressure 2 minutes.

3 When cooking is complete, use quick release. Remove vegetables and tofu to serving bowl with slotted spoon.

4 Stir water into cornstarch in small bowl until smooth. Press Sauté; add cornstarch mixture to pot. Cook and stir 1 minute or until sauce is thickened. Season with salt. Add sauce to bowl with vegetables and tofu; stir gently to coat. Serve over rice.

PEPPERY PORK AND VEGETABLE STEW
MAKES 6 SERVINGS

2 tablespoons olive oil, divided

1½ pounds boneless pork loin, cut into 1-inch pieces

1 package (8 ounces) mushrooms, thickly sliced (1 inch)

1 medium onion, chopped

½ teaspoon dried thyme

½ teaspoon black pepper

½ teaspoon red pepper flakes

¼ teaspoon dried oregano

1 can (about 14 ounces) diced tomatoes

1½ teaspoons salt

1 small butternut squash, peeled and cut into ¾-inch pieces (about 3 cups)

2 red bell peppers, cut into 1-inch pieces

Fresh oregano (optional)

1 Press Sauté; heat 1 tablespoon oil in Instant Pot. Add half of pork; cook 5 minutes or until browned, stirring occasionally. Remove to plate. Repeat with remaining 1 tablespoon oil and pork.

2 Add mushrooms; cook about 3 minutes or until mushrooms begin to release their liquid, stirring occasionally and scraping up browned bits from bottom of pot. Add onion, thyme, black pepper, red pepper flakes and dried oregano; cook and stir 1 minute. Stir in tomatoes, salt and pork; mix well.

3 Secure lid and move pressure release valve to Sealing position. Press Pressure Cook or Manual; cook at high pressure 5 minutes. When cooking is complete, use natural release for 5 minutes, then release remaining pressure.

4 Add squash and bell peppers to pot. Secure lid and move pressure release valve to Sealing position. Press Pressure Cook or Manual; cook at high pressure 3 minutes. When cooking is complete, use quick release. Garnish with fresh oregano.

SWEET POTATO AND BLACK BEAN CHILI
MAKES 6 SERVINGS

1 tablespoon olive oil

1 large onion, chopped

4 teaspoons chili powder

2 cloves garlic, minced

1 teaspoon salt

1 teaspoon chipotle
chili powder

½ teaspoon ground cumin

2 cans (about 15 ounces
each) black beans,
rinsed and drained

1 large sweet potato, peeled
and cut into ½-inch pieces

1 can (about 14 ounces)
diced tomatoes

1 can (about 14 ounces)
crushed tomatoes

1½ cups vegetable broth
or water

Optional toppings: sour
cream, sliced green
onions, shredded
Cheddar cheese
and tortilla strips

1 Press Sauté; heat oil in Instant Pot. Add onion;
cook and stir 3 minutes or until softened. Add
chili powder, garlic, salt, chipotle chili powder
and cumin; cook and stir 1 minute. Stir in beans,
sweet potato, diced tomatoes, crushed tomatoes
and broth; mix well.

2 Secure lid and move pressure release valve
to Sealing position. Press Pressure Cook or
Manual; cook at high pressure 4 minutes.

3 When cooking is complete, use quick release.

4 Press Sauté; cook and stir 3 to 5 minutes or
until chili thickens slightly. Serve with desired
toppings.

QUICK SHRIMP AND OKRA STEW
MAKES 4 SERVINGS

1 tablespoon vegetable oil

½ cup finely chopped onion

8 ounces okra, ends trimmed, cut into ½-inch slices

1 can (about 14 ounces) whole tomatoes, undrained, chopped

1 teaspoon dried thyme

¾ teaspoon salt

8 ounces medium raw shrimp, peeled and deveined

¾ cup fresh corn or thawed frozen corn

½ teaspoon hot pepper sauce

1 Press Sauté; heat oil in Instant Pot. Add onion; cook and stir 2 minutes or until softened. Add okra; cook and stir 3 minutes. Add tomatoes with juice, thyme and salt; mix well.

2 Secure lid and move pressure release valve to Sealing position. Press Pressure Cook or Manual; cook at high pressure 4 minutes.

3 When cooking is complete, use quick release.

4 Press Sauté; add shrimp, corn and hot pepper sauce to pot. Cook 3 minutes or until shrimp are pink and opaque, stirring frequently.

MEXICAN CHICKEN AND BEAN STEW
MAKES 4 TO 6 SERVINGS

1 pound boneless skinless chicken thighs, cut into 1-inch pieces

1 can (about 15 ounces) Great Northern beans, rinsed and drained

1 can (about 15 ounces) black beans, rinsed and drained

1 can (about 14 ounces) crushed tomatoes (preferably fire-roasted)

1 onion, chopped

⅓ cup chicken broth

Juice of 1 large orange (about ⅓ cup)

1 canned chipotle pepper in adobo sauce, minced

1 teaspoon salt

1 teaspoon ground cumin

1 bay leaf

Fresh cilantro sprigs (optional)

1 Combine chicken, beans, tomatoes, onion, broth, orange juice, chipotle pepper, salt, cumin and bay leaf in Instant Pot; mix well.

2 Secure lid and move pressure release valve to Sealing position. Press Pressure Cook or Manual; cook at high pressure 6 minutes.

3 When cooking is complete, use natural release for 5 minutes, then release remaining pressure.

4 Press Sauté; cook 3 to 5 minutes or until stew thickens, stirring frequently. Remove and discard bay leaf. Garnish with cilantro.

Instant Pot®

PULLED CHICKEN SANDWICHES
MAKES 4 SERVINGS

2 pounds boneless skinless chicken thighs

1 small red onion, cut in half and cut into ¼-inch slices

½ cup plus 2 tablespoons barbecue sauce, divided

2 tablespoons water

2 tablespoons Worcestershire sauce

4 pretzel rolls or sandwich buns, split

½ cup cabbage slaw

1 Combine chicken, onion, ½ cup barbecue sauce, water and Worcestershire sauce in Instant Pot; mix well. Secure lid and move pressure release valve to Sealing position. Press Pressure Cook or Manual; cook at high pressure 9 minutes.

2 When cooking is complete, use natural release for 5 minutes, then release remaining pressure. Remove chicken to plate; let stand until cool enough to handle.

3 Meanwhile, press Sauté; cook 5 minutes or until sauce thickens slightly, stirring occasionally. Shred chicken into bite-size pieces; return to pot with remaining 2 tablespoons barbecue sauce. Cook and stir until chicken is coated.

4 Serve chicken mixture on rolls with cabbage slaw.

SHREDDED PORK WRAPS
MAKES 6 SERVINGS

1¼ cups salsa, divided

¼ cup water

1 boneless pork loin roast (about 2 pounds), cut in half crosswise

1 tablespoon cornstarch

6 (8-inch) flour tortillas

3 cups broccoli slaw mix

¾ cup (3 ounces) shredded Cheddar cheese

1 Combine 1 cup salsa and water in Instant Pot; mix well. Add pork; turn to coat. Secure lid and move pressure release valve to Sealing position. Press Pressure Cook or Manual; cook at high pressure 30 minutes.

2 When cooking is complete, use natural release for 10 minutes, then release remaining pressure. Remove pork to plate; let stand until cool enough to handle. Shred or cut pork into bite-size pieces.

3 Stir 2 tablespoons cooking liquid from pot into cornstarch in small bowl until smooth. Press Sauté; add cornstarch mixture and remaining ¼ cup salsa to pot. Cook about 2 minutes or until sauce thickens, stirring constantly. Turn off heat. Remove 1 cup sauce from pot; reserve for dipping. Add pork to pot; stir to coat.

4 Top tortillas with pork, broccoli slaw and cheese. Fold bottom edge of tortillas over filling; fold in sides and roll up to completely to enclose filling. Serve with reserved sauce.

TAVERN BURGER
MAKES 6 SERVINGS

2 pounds ground beef

½ teaspoon salt

⅛ teaspoon black pepper

½ cup water

½ cup ketchup

¼ cup yellow mustard

¼ cup packed brown sugar

6 hamburger buns

1 Press Sauté; add beef to Instant Pot. Cook about 5 minutes or until browned, stirring to break up meat. Drain fat. Season with salt and pepper. Stir in water, ketchup, mustard and brown sugar; mix well.

2 Secure lid and move pressure release valve to Sealing position. Press Pressure Cook or Manual; cook at high pressure 5 minutes.

3 When cooking is complete, use natural release for 5 minutes, then release remaining pressure. Serve beef mixture on buns.

VARIATION

For extra flavor and texture, add a can of pork and beans to the beef with the water and seasonings.

SPEEDY MEATBALL SUBS

MAKES 6 SERVINGS

1 jar (24 ounces) pasta sauce

1 pound frozen Italian-style meatballs

6 sub or hoagie rolls, split

12 slices provolone cheese

Chopped fresh parsley (optional)

1 Pour half of pasta sauce into Instant Pot. Place meatballs in single layer in sauce; top with remaining sauce.

2 Secure lid and move pressure release valve to Sealing position. Press Pressure Cook or Manual; cook at high pressure 11 minutes.

3 Preheat oven to 400°F. Line baking sheet with foil.

4 When cooking is complete, use quick release. Place rolls, cut sides down, on prepared baking sheet. Bake 3 minutes or until lightly toasted.

5 Spoon sauce and meatballs onto bottom halves of rolls; top with cheese slices (two per sandwich). Bake about 3 minutes or until cheese melts. Sprinkle with parsley, if desired; top with top halves of rolls.

MU SHU TURKEY

MAKES 6 SERVINGS

1 jar (about 7 ounces) plum
  sauce, divided

¼ cup orange juice (juice
  of 1 medium orange)

¼ cup finely chopped onion

1 tablespoon minced
  fresh ginger

¼ teaspoon salt

¼ teaspoon ground
  cinnamon

1 pound boneless turkey
  breast or tenderloins,
  cut into thin strips

6 (7-inch) flour tortillas

3 cups coleslaw mix

1 Combine ⅓ cup plum sauce, orange juice, onion,
  ginger, salt and cinnamon in Instant Pot; mix well.
  Add turkey, stir to coat.

2 Secure lid and move pressure release valve
  to Sealing position. Press Pressure Cook or
  Manual; cook at high pressure 4 minutes.

3 When cooking is complete, use quick release.

4 Press Sauté; cook 2 to 3 minutes or until sauce
  is reduced and thickens slightly.

5 Spread remaining jarred plum sauce over tortillas;
  top with turkey and coleslaw mix. Roll up to
  enclose filling. Serve with remaining cooking
  liquid for dipping.

ITALIAN BEEF SANDWICHES
MAKES 4 SERVINGS

1 jar (16 ounces) sliced
   pepperoncini peppers

1 jar (16 ounces) giardiniera

2 to 2½ pounds boneless
   beef chuck roast

½ cup beef broth

1 tablespoon Italian
   seasoning

4 French or sub rolls, split

1 Drain pepperoncini, reserving ½ cup liquid. Set aside ½ cup pepperoncini for sandwiches. Drain giardiniera, reserving ½ cup vegetables for sandwiches.

2 Combine beef, remaining pepperoncini and reserved ½ cup pepperoncini liquid, remaining giardiniera vegetables, broth and Italian seasoning in Instant Pot.

3 Secure lid and move pressure release valve to Sealing position. Press Pressure Cook or Manual; cook at high pressure 60 minutes.

4 When cooking is complete, use natural release for 15 minutes, then release remaining pressure. Remove beef to large bowl; let stand until cool enough to handle. Shred beef into bite-size pieces. Add ½ cup cooking liquid; toss to coat.

5 Fill rolls with beef, reserved pepperoncini and reserved giardiniera vegetables. Serve with warm cooking liquid for dipping.

HOISIN BARBECUE CHICKEN SLIDERS

MAKES 16 SLIDERS

⅔ cup hoisin sauce

⅓ cup barbecue sauce

1 tablespoon soy sauce

¼ teaspoon red pepper flakes

3 to 3½ pounds boneless skinless chicken thighs

2 tablespoons water

1 tablespoon cornstarch

16 dinner rolls or Hawaiian rolls, split

½ medium red onion, finely chopped

Sliced pickles (optional)

1 Combine hoisin sauce, barbecue sauce, soy sauce and red pepper flakes in Instant Pot; mix well. Add chicken; stir to coat.

2 Secure lid and move pressure release valve to Sealing position. Press Pressure Cook or Manual; cook at high pressure 8 minutes.

3 When cooking is complete, use natural release for 5 minutes, then release remaining pressure.

4 Remove chicken to large plate; let stand until cool enough to handle. Shred chicken into bite-size pieces.

5 Stir water into cornstarch in small bowl until smooth. Press Sauté; add cornstarch mixture to pot. Cook and stir about 2 minutes or until sauce thickens. Return chicken to pot; mix well.

6 Spoon about ¼ cup chicken mixture onto each roll; serve with onion and pickles, if desired.

CHORIZO BURRITOS
MAKES 4 SERVINGS

14 ounces uncooked Mexican chorizo sausages, cut into bite-size pieces

2 green or red bell peppers, cut into 1-inch pieces

1 can (about 15 ounces) kidney or pinto beans, rinsed and drained

1 can (about 14 ounces) diced tomatoes

1 can (11 ounces) corn, drained

½ teaspoon ground cumin

½ teaspoon ground cinnamon

8 (8-inch) flour tortillas, warmed

2 cups hot cooked rice

1 cup (4 ounces) shredded Monterey Jack cheese

1 Combine chorizo, bell peppers, beans, tomatoes, corn, cumin and cinnamon in Instant Pot; mix well.

2 Secure lid and move pressure release valve to Sealing position. Press Pressure Cook or Manual; cook at high pressure 10 minutes.

3 When cooking is complete, use natural release for 10 minutes, then release remaining pressure.

4 Press Sauté; cook about 5 minutes or until chorizo mixture thickens, stirring occasionally.

5 Spoon chorizo mixture down centers of tortillas; top with rice and cheese. Roll up tortillas; serve immediately.

CHIPOTLE BBQ TURKEY SANDWICHES

MAKES 4 SERVINGS

1 tablespoon vegetable oil

1 small red onion, chopped

½ teaspoon chipotle chili powder

¾ cup plus 2 tablespoons barbecue sauce, divided

1 package (24 ounces) turkey tenderloins (2 tenderloins), each cut in half

4 sandwich buns

1 Press Sauté; heat oil in Instant Pot. Add onion; cook and stir 3 minutes or until softened. Add chili powder; cook and stir 30 seconds. Stir in ¾ cup barbecue sauce; mix well. Add turkey; turn to coat.

2 Secure lid and move pressure release valve to Sealing position. Press Pressure Cook or Manual; cook at high pressure 20 minutes.

3 When cooking is complete, use natural release for 10 minutes, then release remaining pressure. Remove turkey to plate; let stand 5 minutes or until cool enough to handle. Shred turkey into bite-size pieces.

4 Meanwhile, press Sauté; adjust heat to low. Cook sauce 5 minutes or until slightly reduced. Add shredded turkey and remaining 2 tablespoons barbecue sauce to pot; cook 2 minutes, stirring frequently. Serve on buns.

HOT AND SWEET SAUSAGE SANDWICHES
MAKES 5 SERVINGS

1½ cups pasta sauce

1 large sweet onion, cut into ¼-inch slices

1 medium green bell pepper, cut into ½-inch slices

1 medium red bell pepper, cut into ½-inch slices

1½ tablespoons packed dark brown sugar

1 package (16 ounces) hot Italian sausage links (5 links)

5 Italian rolls, split

1 Combine pasta sauce, onion, bell peppers and brown sugar in Instant Pot; mix well. Add sausages to pot; spoon some of sauce mixture over sausages.

2 Secure lid and move pressure release valve to Sealing position. Press Pressure Cook or Manual; cook at high pressure 5 minutes.

3 When cooking is complete, use natural release for 10 minutes, then release remaining pressure. Remove sausages to plate; tent with foil.

4 Press Sauté; cook 10 minutes or until sauce is reduced by one third, stirring occasionally. Serve sausages in rolls; top with sauce.

TIP

If you have leftover sauce, refrigerate or freeze it and serve over pasta or polenta. Top with grated Parmesan cheese.

TUESDAY NIGHT TACOS
MAKES 4 TO 6 SERVINGS

1 tablespoon vegetable oil

1½ pounds boneless skinless chicken thighs

1 cup chunky salsa

Corn tortillas, warmed

½ cup shredded lettuce

1 cup pico de gallo

1 cup (4 ounces) shredded taco blend or Cheddar cheese

Lime wedges (optional)

Optional toppings: sour cream, sliced jalapeño peppers, pickled onions and/or diced avocado

1 Press Sauté; heat oil in Instant Pot. Add chicken; cook 5 minutes or until browned on both sides.

2 Add salsa; cook 1 minute, scraping up browned bits from bottom of pot. Turn chicken to coat with salsa.

3 Secure lid and move pressure release valve to Sealing position. Press Pressure Cook or Manual; cook at high pressure 11 minutes.

4 When cooking is complete, use quick release. Let stand 5 minutes; use two forks or tongs to shred chicken into bite-size pieces in pot.

5 Serve chicken mixture in tortillas with lettuce, pico de gallo, cheese and lime wedges, if desired. Top as desired.

Instant Pot

PERFECT BBQ RIBS
MAKES 4 SERVINGS

1 rack pork baby back ribs (about 3 pounds)

⅓ cup barbecue seasoning or grilling rub

2 cups apple juice

¼ cup cider vinegar

1 tablespoon liquid smoke

1 cup barbecue sauce, plus additional for serving

1 Remove membrane covering bones on underside of ribs. Rub barbecue seasoning generously over both sides of ribs, pressing to adhere.

2 Combine apple juice, vinegar and liquid smoke in Instant Pot; mix well. Stand ribs vertically in liquid, coiling ribs into a ring to fit in pot.

3 Secure lid and move pressure release valve to Sealing position. Press Pressure Cook or Manual; cook at high pressure 20 minutes. Preheat broiler. Line baking sheet with foil.

4 When cooking is complete, use natural release for 5 minutes, then release remaining pressure. Remove ribs to prepared baking sheet, meaty side up. Brush both sides of ribs with 1 cup barbecue sauce.

5 Broil 5 minutes or until sauce begins to bubble and char. Serve ribs with additional sauce.

CHICKEN AND SAUSAGE JAMBALAYA
MAKES 6 TO 8 SERVINGS

1 tablespoon vegetable oil

12 ounces andouille sausage or other smoked sausage, cut into ¼-inch slices

12 ounces boneless skinless chicken breast, cut into 1-inch pieces

1 onion, chopped

½ red bell pepper, diced

½ green bell pepper, diced

4 cloves garlic, minced

1½ tablespoons Cajun seasoning

¾ teaspoon dried thyme

1 can (about 14 ounces) diced tomatoes

1½ cups uncooked rice, rinsed well and drained

¾ cup chicken broth

2 bay leaves

Sliced green onions or chopped fresh parsley (optional)

1 Press Sauté; heat oil in Instant Pot. Add sausage; cook about 5 minutes or until browned, stirring occasionally. Remove to plate.

2 Add chicken to pot; cook and stir 3 minutes or just until outside of chicken is no longer pink. Add onion, bell peppers, garlic, Cajun seasoning and thyme; cook 2 minutes, scraping up browned bits from bottom of pot.

3 Return sausage to pot; stir in tomatoes, rice, broth and bay leaves. Secure lid and move pressure release valve to Sealing position. Press Pressure Cook or Manual; cook at high pressure 7 minutes.

4 When cooking is complete, use natural release for 10 minutes, then release remaining pressure. Stir rice; remove and discard bay leaves. Top with green onions, if desired.

SHORTCUT SPANISH TORTILLA
MAKES 4 TO 6 SERVINGS

2 tablespoons olive oil

1 small onion, cut in half
 and thinly sliced

8 eggs

¼ teaspoon salt

⅛ teaspoon black pepper

4 ounces potato chips
 (use plain thin chips, not
 kettle), lightly crushed

1½ cups water

 Chopped fresh chives
 or parsley (optional)

1 Spray 7-inch round metal cake pan with nonstick cooking spray. Press Sauté; heat oil in Instant Pot. Add onion; cook and stir about 4 minutes or until softened and beginning to brown. Remove to small bowl; set aside to cool 5 minutes. Wipe out pot with paper towel.

2 Meanwhile, beat eggs, salt and pepper in medium bowl until blended. Add potato chips; fold in gently until all chips are coated. Let stand 5 minutes to soften. Stir in onion until well blended. Pour egg mixture into prepared pan; smooth top.

3 Pour water into pot; place rack in pot. Place pan on rack. Secure lid and move pressure release valve to Sealing position. Press Pressure Cook or Manual; cook at high pressure 20 minutes.

4 When cooking is complete, use quick release. Remove pan to wire rack to cool 5 minutes.

5 Invert tortilla onto plate; invert again onto serving plate or cutting board. Serve warm or at room temperature; garnish with chives.

TURKEY STROGANOFF
MAKES 4 SERVINGS

1 tablespoon olive oil

4 cups sliced mushrooms

2 stalks celery, sliced

2 medium shallots *or*
 ½ small onion, minced

2 turkey tenderloins
 (about 5 ounces each),
 cut into 1-inch pieces

¼ cup chicken broth

1½ tablespoons
 Worcestershire sauce

¾ teaspoon salt

½ teaspoon dried thyme

¼ teaspoon black pepper

½ cup sour cream

1 tablespoon all-purpose
 flour

 Hot cooked egg noodles

1 Press Sauté; heat oil in Instant Pot. Add mushrooms, celery and shallots; cook and stir 5 minutes or until vegetables are softened. Add turkey, broth, Worcestershire sauce, salt, thyme and pepper; mix well.

2 Secure lid and move pressure release valve to Sealing position. Press Pressure Cook or Manual; cook at high pressure 6 minutes.

3 When cooking is complete, use natural release for 5 minutes, then release remaining pressure.

4 Combine sour cream and flour in small bowl; stir in ¼ cup hot cooking liquid from pot until smooth.

5 Press Sauté; add sour cream mixture to pot. Cook and stir 3 minutes or until sauce thickens. Serve over noodles.

BUTTER CHICKEN
MAKES 4 TO 6 SERVINGS

2 tablespoons butter

1 onion, chopped

4 cloves garlic, minced

1 teaspoon minced
   fresh ginger

1 teaspoon ground turmeric

1 teaspoon ground
   coriander

1 teaspoon garam masala

1 teaspoon ground cumin

½ teaspoon ground
   red pepper

½ teaspoon paprika

1 can (about 14 ounces)
   diced tomatoes

¾ teaspoon salt

2 pounds boneless skinless
   chicken breasts, cut
   into 2-inch pieces

½ cup whipping cream

Chopped fresh cilantro

Hot cooked rice (optional)

1 Press Sauté; melt butter in Instant Pot. Add onion; cook and stir about 4 minutes or until onion begins to turn golden. Add garlic and ginger; cook and stir 1 minute. Add turmeric, coriander, garam masala, cumin, red pepper and paprika; cook and stir 30 seconds. Add tomatoes and salt; cook and stir 2 minutes. Stir in chicken; mix well.

2 Secure lid and move pressure release valve to Sealing position. Press Pressure Cook or Manual; cook at high pressure 8 minutes.

3 When cooking is complete, use natural release for 10 minutes, then release remaining pressure.

4 Press Sauté; adjust heat to low. Stir in cream; cook 5 minutes or until heated through. Sprinkle with cilantro; serve with rice, if desired.

SHAKSHUKA
MAKES 4 SERVINGS

2 tablespoons extra virgin olive oil

1 large red bell pepper, chopped

1 medium onion, chopped

3 cloves garlic, minced

2 teaspoons sugar

2 teaspoons ground cumin

1 teaspoon paprika

1 teaspoon chili powder

½ teaspoon salt

¼ teaspoon red pepper flakes

1 can (28 ounces) crushed tomatoes

¾ cup (3 ounces) crumbled feta cheese

4 eggs

1 Press Sauté; heat oil in Instant Pot. Add bell pepper and onion; cook and stir 3 minutes or until vegetables are softened. Add garlic, sugar, cumin, paprika, chili powder, salt and red pepper flakes; cook and stir 1 minute. Stir in tomatoes; mix well.

2 Secure lid and move pressure release valve to Sealing position. Press Pressure Cook or Manual; cook at high pressure 10 minutes.

3 When cooking is complete, use quick release.

4 Stir in cheese. Make four wells in sauce for eggs, leaving space between each. Slide eggs, one at a time, into wells in sauce. (For best results, crack each egg into small bowl before sliding into sauce.)

5 Secure lid and move pressure release valve to Sealing position. Press Pressure Cook or Manual; cook at low pressure 1 minute. When cooking is complete, use quick release. To cook eggs longer, press Sauté and cook until desired doneness.

PORK PICADILLO

MAKES 4 SERVINGS

- 1 tablespoon olive oil
- 1 pound boneless pork country-style ribs, trimmed and cut into ½-inch pieces
- 1 onion, chopped
- 2 cloves garlic, minced
- 1 can (about 14 ounces) diced tomatoes
- ½ cup raisins
- 2 tablespoons cider vinegar
- 2 canned chipotle peppers in adobo sauce, chopped
- ½ teaspoon salt
- ½ teaspoon ground cumin
- ½ teaspoon ground cinnamon

1. Press Sauté; heat oil in Instant Pot. Add pork; cook about 6 minutes or until browned, stirring occasionally. Add onion; cook and stir 2 minutes. Add garlic; cook and stir 30 seconds. Stir in tomatoes, raisins, vinegar, chipotle peppers, salt, cumin and cinnamon, scraping up browned bits from bottom of pot.
2. Secure lid and move pressure release valve to Sealing position. Press Pressure Cook or Manual; cook at high pressure 25 minutes.
3. When cooking is complete, use natural release for 10 minutes, then release remaining pressure. Stir pork mixture with tongs, breaking up pork into smaller pieces.

SERVING SUGGESTION

Serve with hot cooked rice or tortillas.

ARTICHOKE DIJON CHICKEN THIGHS
MAKES 4 TO 6 SERVINGS

1 jar (12 ounces) quartered marinated artichoke hearts, undrained

⅓ cup Dijon mustard

2 tablespoons minced garlic

½ teaspoon dried tarragon

¼ teaspoon salt

2½ pounds bone-in chicken thighs, skin removed

1½ cups thickly sliced mushrooms

1 cup chopped onion

2 tablespoons water

1 tablespoon all-purpose flour

¼ cup chopped fresh parsley

Hot cooked pasta (optional)

1 Drain artichokes, reserving ½ cup marinade. Discard remaining marinade. Combine reserved marinade, mustard, garlic, tarragon and salt in Instant Pot; mix well. Add chicken, mushrooms and onion; stir to coat.

2 Secure lid and move pressure release valve to Sealing position. Press Pressure Cook or Manual; cook at high pressure 11 minutes.

3 When cooking is complete, use natural release for 10 minutes, then release remaining pressure.

4 Remove chicken to plate; tent with foil to keep warm. Press Sauté; add artichokes to pot. Cook about 5 minutes or until sauce is reduced by half and artichokes are heated through, stirring occasionally.

5 Stir water into flour in small bowl until smooth. Add to sauce; cook and stir 1 minute or until sauce thickens. Stir in parsley. Serve chicken and sauce over pasta, if desired.

CRUSTLESS SPINACH QUICHE
MAKES 6 SERVINGS

6 eggs

¾ cup half-and-half

¾ teaspoon Italian seasoning

½ teaspoon salt

½ teaspoon black pepper

1 package (10 ounces) frozen chopped spinach, thawed and squeezed dry

1 cup (4 ounces) shredded Italian cheese blend

1½ cups water

1 Spray 7-inch round metal cake pan with nonstick cooking spray. Beat eggs, half-and-half, Italian seasoning, salt and pepper in medium bowl until well blended. Stir in spinach and cheese; mix well. Pour into prepared pan; cover with foil.

2 Pour water into Instant Pot; place rack in pot. Place pan on rack.

3 Secure lid and move pressure release valve to Sealing position. Press Pressure Cook or Manual; cook at high pressure 28 minutes.

4 When cooking is complete, use natural release for 5 minutes, then release remaining pressure. Remove pan from pot. Uncover; let stand 5 minutes before serving.

TIP

To remove the quiche from the pan for serving, run a knife around the edge of the pan to loosen. Invert the quiche onto a plate; invert again onto a second plate. Cut into wedges to serve.

INSTANT CHICKEN ADOBO
MAKES 4 SERVINGS

⅓ cup cider vinegar

⅓ cup reduced-sodium soy sauce

5 cloves garlic, minced

3 bay leaves

1 teaspoon black pepper

2½ pounds bone-in skin-on chicken thighs

Hot cooked rice (optional)

Sliced green onion (optional)

1 Combine vinegar, soy sauce, garlic, bay leaves and pepper in Instant Pot; mix well. Add chicken; turn to coat. Arrange chicken skin side down in liquid.

2 Secure lid and move pressure release valve to Sealing position. Press Pressure Cook or Manual; cook at high pressure 13 minutes.

3 Preheat broiler. Line baking sheet with foil.

4 When cooking is complete, use natural release for 10 minutes, then release remaining pressure. Remove chicken to prepared baking sheet, skin side up.

5 Broil chicken about 4 minutes or until skin is browned and crisp. Meanwhile, press Sauté; cook liquid in pot about 5 minutes or until slightly reduced.

6 Pour sauce over chicken; serve with rice, if desired. Garnish with green onion.

EASY MEATBALLS
MAKES 4 SERVINGS

1 pound ground beef

1 egg, beaten

3 tablespoons Italian-seasoned dry bread crumbs

1 clove garlic, minced

1 teaspoon dried oregano

¾ teaspoon salt

¼ teaspoon black pepper

⅛ teaspoon ground red pepper

3 cups marinara or tomato-basil pasta sauce

Hot cooked spaghetti

Slivered fresh basil (optional)

Grated Parmesan cheese (optional)

1 Combine beef, egg, bread crumbs, garlic, oregano, salt, black pepper and red pepper in medium bowl; mix gently. Shape into 16 (1½-inch) meatballs.

2 Pour marinara sauce into Instant Pot. Add meatballs to sauce; turn to coat and submerge meatballs in sauce.

3 Secure lid and move pressure release valve to Sealing position. Press Pressure Cook or Manual; cook at high pressure 8 minutes.

4 When cooking is complete, use quick release. Serve meatballs and sauce over spaghetti; top with basil and cheese, if desired.

HERB LEMON TURKEY BREAST
MAKES 4 SERVINGS

½ **cup lemon juice**

½ **cup dry white wine**

4 **cloves garlic, minced**

1 **teaspoon salt**

½ **teaspoon dried parsley flakes**

½ **teaspoon dried tarragon**

½ **teaspoon dried rosemary**

¼ **teaspoon ground sage**

¼ **teaspoon black pepper**

1 **boneless turkey breast (about 3 pounds)**

Fresh rosemary sprigs and lemon slices (optional)

1 Combine lemon juice, wine, garlic, salt, parsley flakes, tarragon, dried rosemary, sage and pepper in measuring cup or small bowl; mix well.

2 Place turkey breast in Instant Pot; pour juice mixture over turkey, turning to coat. (Turkey should be skin side up for cooking.)

3 Secure lid and move pressure release valve to Sealing position. Press Pressure Cook or Manual; cook at high pressure 30 minutes.

4 When cooking is complete, use natural release for 10 minutes, then release remaining pressure. Remove turkey to cutting board; tent with foil to keep warm. Let stand 10 minutes before slicing.

5 Use cooking liquid as sauce, if desired, or thicken liquid with flour (see Tip). Garnish with fresh rosemary and lemon slices.

TIP

If desired, prepare gravy with cooking liquid after removing turkey from pot. Place ¼ cup all-purpose flour in small bowl; stir in ½ cup cooking liquid from pot until smooth. Press Sauté; add flour mixture to pot. Cook 5 minutes or until gravy thickens, stirring frequently.

SIMPLE CHINESE CHICKEN
MAKES 4 SERVINGS

1 cut-up whole chicken
  (3 to 3½ pounds)

¼ cup dry sherry

¼ cup reduced-sodium
  soy sauce

4 cloves garlic, minced

1 tablespoon minced
  fresh ginger

¼ teaspoon red pepper
  flakes

1 Place chicken in large resealable food storage bag. Combine sherry, soy sauce, garlic, ginger and red pepper flakes in small bowl; mix well. Pour over chicken; seal bag and turn to coat. Marinate chicken in refrigerator at least 30 minutes or up to 4 hours, turning once or twice.

2 Place chicken and marinade in Instant Pot. Secure lid and move pressure release valve to Sealing position. Press Pressure Cook or Manual; cook at high pressure 13 minutes.

3 Preheat broiler. Line large baking sheet with foil.

4 When cooking is complete, use natural release for 10 minutes, then release remaining pressure.

5 Place chicken on prepared baking sheet, skin side up. Broil 5 to 7 minutes or until skin is browned and crisp, basting once with cooking liquid from pot.

Instant Pot®

PASTA

SOUTHWESTERN MAC AND CHEESE
MAKES 6 TO 8 SERVINGS

4 tablespoons (½ stick) butter, divided

1 onion, finely chopped

3⅓ cups water

1 package (16 ounces) uncooked elbow macaroni

1 can (about 14 ounces) diced tomatoes with green peppers and onions

1 teaspoon salt

4 cups (16 ounces) shredded Mexican cheese blend, divided

½ cup milk

1 cup salsa

1 Press Sauté; melt 1 tablespoon butter in Instant Pot. Add onion; cook and stir 3 minutes or until softened. Stir in water, macaroni, tomatoes and salt; mix well.

2 Secure lid and move pressure release valve to Sealing position. Press Pressure Cook or Manual; cook at high pressure 4 minutes.

3 When cooking is complete, use quick release.

4 Press Sauté; add 3½ cups cheese, milk and remaining 3 tablespoons butter to pot. Stir until smooth and well blended. Stir in salsa. Turn off heat. Sprinkle remaining ½ cup cheese over pasta; cover and let stand until melted.

ONE-POT PASTA WITH SAUSAGE
MAKES 6 SERVINGS

1 tablespoon olive oil

1 pound smoked sausage (about 4 links), cut into ¼-inch slices

1 onion, diced

1 tablespoon tomato paste

2 cloves garlic, minced

1½ teaspoons dried oregano

¼ teaspoon red pepper flakes

1 can (28 ounces) whole tomatoes, undrained, crushed with hands or coarsely chopped

2½ cups water

1½ teaspoons salt

1 package (16 ounces) uncooked cellentani pasta

1½ cups frozen peas

½ cup shredded Parmesan cheese

⅓ cup shredded fresh basil, plus additional for garnish

1 Press Sauté; heat oil in Instant Pot. Add sausage; cook about 7 minutes or until browned, stirring occasionally. Add onion; cook and stir 3 minutes or until softened. Add tomato paste, garlic, oregano and red pepper flakes; cook and stir 1 minute. Add tomatoes with juice, water and salt; cook 2 minutes, scraping up browned bits from bottom of pot. Stir in pasta; mix well.

2 Secure lid and move pressure release valve to Sealing position. Press Pressure Cook or Manual; cook at high pressure 5 minutes.

3 When cooking is complete, use quick release.

4 Press Sauté; add peas to pot. Cook and stir 2 minutes. Turn off heat; stir in cheese and ⅓ cup basil. Cover and let stand 2 minutes. Garnish with additional basil.

VARIATION

You can substitute 1 pound uncooked Italian sausage for the smoked sausage. Remove the casings, cut into ½-inch pieces and proceed with the recipe as directed.

PENNE WITH RICOTTA, TOMATOES AND BASIL
MAKES 4 SERVINGS

2 cans (about 14 ounces each) diced tomatoes with basil, garlic and oregano

2½ cups water

3 teaspoons salt, divided

1 package (16 ounces) uncooked penne pasta

1 container (15 ounces) ricotta cheese

⅔ cup chopped fresh basil

¼ cup extra virgin olive oil

1 tablespoon balsamic vinegar

1 clove garlic, minced

¼ teaspoon black pepper

Grated Parmesan cheese

1 Combine tomatoes, water and 2 teaspoons salt in Instant Pot; mix well. Stir in pasta.

2 Secure lid and move pressure release valve to Sealing position. Press Pressure Cook or Manual; cook at high pressure 5 minutes.

3 Meanwhile, combine ricotta, basil, oil, vinegar, garlic, remaining 1 teaspoon salt and pepper in medium bowl; mix well.

4 When cooking is complete, use quick release. Drain any remaining liquid in pot. Add ricotta mixture to pot; stir gently to coat. Sprinkle with Parmesan just before serving.

ASIAN CHICKEN AND NOODLES
MAKES 4 SERVINGS

1 tablespoon vegetable oil

1 pound boneless skinless chicken breasts, cut into 1×½-inch pieces

1 bottle or jar (about 12 ounces) stir-fry sauce

¾ cup chicken broth or water

8 ounces uncooked thin Pad Thai rice noodles (⅛ inch wide)

1 package (16 ounces) frozen stir-fry vegetable blend (do not thaw)

1 Press Sauté; heat oil in Instant Pot. Add chicken; cook about 4 minutes or until no longer pink, stirring occasionally.

2 Stir in stir-fry sauce and broth; mix well. Top with noodles, breaking to fit as necessary. Cover with vegetables in even layer. (Do not stir.)

3 Secure lid and move pressure release valve to Sealing position. Press Pressure Cook or Manual; cook at high pressure 2 minutes.

4 When cooking is complete, use quick release. Stir with tongs to separate noodles and coat noodles and vegetables with sauce. If there is excess liquid in pot, press Sauté; cook and stir 2 minutes or until liquid has evaporated.

CHILI WAGON WHEEL PASTA
MAKES 4 SERVINGS

1 tablespoon olive oil

1 pound ground turkey
   or ground beef

1 cup chopped onion

1 green bell pepper,
   chopped

2 teaspoons salt

2 teaspoons chili powder

½ teaspoon dried oregano

½ teaspoon black pepper

¼ teaspoon ground allspice

1 can (about 14 ounces)
   diced tomatoes

1 can (8 ounces)
   tomato sauce

½ cup water

8 ounces uncooked mini
   wagon wheel pasta

1 cup (4 ounces) shredded
   Cheddar cheese

1 Press Sauté; heat oil in Instant Pot. Add turkey; cook 5 minutes or until no longer pink, stirring frequently. Add onion and bell pepper; cook and stir 3 minutes or until vegetables are softened. Add salt, chili powder, oregano, black pepper and allspice; cook and stir 30 seconds. Stir in tomatoes, tomato sauce and water; mix well. Stir in pasta.

2 Secure lid and move pressure release valve to Sealing position. Press Pressure Cook or Manual; cook at high pressure 4 minutes.

3 When cooking is complete, use quick release. Stir in cheese.

ORECCHIETTE WITH SAUSAGE AND BROCCOLI RABE
MAKES 4 TO 6 SERVINGS

1 tablespoon olive oil

12 ounces bulk mild Italian sausage

1 bunch broccoli rabe (about 1 pound), tough stems removed, cut into 2-inch-long pieces

3 cloves garlic, minced

¼ teaspoon red pepper flakes

¼ cup dry white wine

1 package (16 ounces) uncooked orecchiette pasta

4 cups chicken broth

⅓ cup water

1 teaspoon salt

¾ cup grated Parmesan cheese, divided

Juice of 1 lemon

1 Press Sauté; heat oil in Instant Pot. Add sausage; cook about 8 minutes or until browned, stirring to break up meat. Remove to plate with slotted spoon. Add broccoli rabe to pot; cook and stir 5 minutes or until crisp-tender. Remove to bowl; cover with foil to keep warm.

2 Return sausage to pot. Add garlic and red pepper flakes; cook and stir 1 minute. Add wine; cook 2 minutes, scraping up browned bits from bottom of pot. Stir in pasta, broth, water and salt; mix well, separating pasta pieces as much as possible. (Orchiette pasta often sticks together in stacks in the package and during cooking.)

3 Secure lid and move pressure release valve to Sealing position. Press Pressure Cook or Manual; cook at high pressure 5 minutes.

4 When cooking is complete, use quick release. Stir in broccoli rabe, ½ cup cheese and lemon juice; mix well. Serve immediately with remaining cheese.

PENNE WITH CHUNKY TOMATO SAUCE AND SPINACH
MAKES 4 SERVINGS

1 tablespoon olive oil

1 cup chopped onion

2 cloves garlic, minced

2 teaspoons salt

½ teaspoon dried oregano

½ teaspoon dried basil

¼ teaspoon red pepper flakes

¼ teaspoon black pepper

1 can (6 ounces) tomato paste

2 cups water

8 ounces uncooked penne pasta

1 package (5 ounces) baby spinach

1 large ripe tomato, seeded and chopped

¼ cup grated Parmesan cheese

¼ cup chopped fresh basil

1 Press Sauté; heat oil in Instant Pot. Add onion and garlic; cook and stir 3 minutes or until softened. Add salt, oregano, dried basil, red pepper flakes and black pepper; cook and stir 30 seconds. Add tomato paste; cook and stir 1 minute. Add water; stir until well blended. Stir in pasta; mix well.

2 Secure lid and move pressure release valve to Sealing position. Press Pressure Cook or Manual; cook at high pressure 4 minutes.

3 When cooking is complete, use quick release. Stir in spinach and tomato; cover and let stand 2 to 3 minutes or until spinach is wilted. Top with cheese and fresh basil.

INSTANT SPAGHETTI AND MEATBALLS
MAKES 6 SERVINGS

1 pound frozen meatballs

8 ounces uncooked spaghetti, broken in half

1 tablespoon olive oil

¾ teaspoon salt

2 cups water

1 jar (24 ounces) chunky marinara sauce

Grated Parmesan cheese and fresh basil leaves (optional)

1 Place meatballs in Instant Pot in single layer. Arrange pasta in criss-crossing layers over meatballs; drizzle with oil.

2 Stir salt into water in measuring cup. Pour marinara sauce and water over pasta, making sure to cover pasta completely. (Do not stir.)

3 Secure lid and move pressure release valve to Sealing position. Press Pressure Cook or Manual; cook at high pressure 9 minutes.

4 When cooking is complete, use quick release. Gently stir with tongs to separate pasta and blend with sauce. Garnish with cheese and basil.

PASTA E CECI
MAKES 4 SERVINGS

1 cup dried chickpeas,
  soaked 8 hours
  or overnight

3 tablespoons olive oil

1 onion, chopped

1 carrot, chopped

2 teaspoons salt

1 clove garlic, minced

1 teaspoon minced fresh
  rosemary

1 can (28 ounces) whole
  tomatoes, undrained,
  crushed with hands
  or coarsely chopped

2 cups vegetable broth
  or water

1 bay leaf

⅛ teaspoon red pepper
  flakes

1 cup uncooked
  orecchiette pasta

  Black pepper

  Chopped fresh parsley
  (optional)

1 Drain and rinse chickpeas. Press Sauté; heat oil in Instant Pot. Add onion and carrot; cook and stir 8 minutes or until vegetables are softened. Add salt, garlic and rosemary; cook and stir 1 minute. Add chickpeas, tomatoes with juice, broth, bay leaf and red pepper flakes; mix well.

2 Secure lid and move pressure release valve to Sealing position. Press Pressure Cook or Manual; cook at high pressure 15 minutes. When cooking is complete, use natural release for 5 minutes, then release remaining pressure.

3 Stir in pasta. Secure lid and move pressure release valve to Sealing position. Press Pressure Cook or Manual; cook at high pressure 6 minutes.

4 When cooking is complete, use quick release. Remove and discard bay leaf. Season with black pepper; garnish with parsley.

TIP

To crush the tomatoes, take them out of the can one at a time and crush them between your fingers over the pot. Or coarsely chop them with a knife.

CHICKEN WITH PARMESAN FETTUCCINE
MAKES 4 SERVINGS

1 pound boneless skinless chicken breasts, cut into 1-inch pieces

1 teaspoon salt, divided

¼ teaspoon black pepper

2 tablespoons butter, divided

1 clove garlic, minced

1½ cups chicken broth

8 ounces uncooked fettuccine, broken in half

⅔ cup whipping cream

½ cup grated Parmesan cheese

½ cup chopped green onions

1 Season chicken with ½ teaspoon salt and pepper. Press Sauté; melt 1 tablespoon butter in Instant Pot. Add chicken and garlic; cook 5 minutes without stirring. Cook and stir 1 minute; remove chicken to medium bowl. Add broth to pot; cook 1 minute, scraping up browned bits from bottom of pot.

2 Add pasta and remaining ½ teaspoon salt to pot, pressing pasta down into broth. Top with chicken. (Do not stir.)

3 Secure lid and move pressure release valve to Sealing position. Press Pressure Cook or Manual; cook at high pressure 5 minutes.

4 When cooking is complete, use quick release. Stir in cream and remaining 1 tablespoon butter; cook 3 to 4 minutes or until pasta is al dente and most of liquid is absorbed. Gradually add cheese, stirring until blended. Stir in green onions.

VARIATION

Just before serving, stir in steamed asparagus pieces or other steamed vegetable; stir to coat.

TURKEY VEGETABLE CHILI MAC
MAKES 6 SERVINGS

1 tablespoon vegetable oil

1 pound ground turkey

1 cup chopped onion

2 cloves garlic, minced

1 can (about 15 ounces) black beans, rinsed and drained

1 can (about 14 ounces) diced tomatoes with onion and bell pepper

1 can (about 14 ounces) diced tomatoes

1½ cups water

1 cup uncooked elbow macaroni

1 teaspoon salt

1 teaspoon chili powder

½ teaspoon ground cumin

1 cup frozen corn

Sour cream (optional)

1 Press Sauté; heat oil in Instant Pot. Add turkey, onion and garlic; cook and stir 5 minutes or until turkey is no longer pink. Stir in beans, tomatoes, water, macaroni, salt, chili powder and cumin; mix well.

2 Secure lid and move pressure release valve to Sealing position. Press Pressure Cook or Manual; cook at high pressure 3 minutes.

3 When cooking is complete, use quick release.

4 Press Sauté; add corn to pot. Cook about 2 minutes or until corn is heated through and any excess liquid is absorbed, stirring occasionally. Serve with sour cream, if desired.

TIP

You can substitute 2 ounces of any other pasta for the elbow macaroni. Short pasta shapes like cavatappi, penne or rigatoni (which are sometimes called "cut pastas" because they are cut into pieces during the manufacturing process) can be added straight out of the packages. Longer shapes such as linguine, fettuccine or spaghetti should be broken in halves or thirds before being stirred in so that all the pasta can be fully immersed in the sauce.

SPICY SAUSAGE AND PENNE PASTA
MAKES 4 TO 6 SERVINGS

- 1 pound uncooked bulk hot Italian sausage
- 1 cup chopped onion
- 2 cloves garlic, minced
- 2 teaspoons salt
- 1 teaspoon dried oregano
- 1 teaspoon dried basil
- 2 cans (about 14 ounces each) diced tomatoes
- 1½ cups water
- 8 ounces uncooked penne pasta
- 3 cups broccoli florets (from 1 medium head)
- ½ cup shredded Asiago or Romano cheese

1 Press Sauté; crumble sausage into Instant Pot. Add onion; cook 10 minutes or until sausage is cooked through, stirring frequently. Add garlic, salt, oregano and basil; cook and stir 1 minute. Stir in tomatoes, water and pasta; mix well.

2 Secure lid and move pressure release valve to Sealing position. Press Pressure Cook or Manual; cook at high pressure 3 minutes.

3 When cooking is complete, use quick release. Stir in broccoli. Secure lid and move pressure release valve to Sealing position. Press Pressure Cook or Manual; cook at high pressure 0 minutes. (Set cooking time for 0 minutes; Instant Pot will beep as soon as contents reach pressure.)

4 When cooking is complete, use quick release. Stir pasta; sprinkle with cheese.

Instant Pot

VEGETABLES

GARLIC PARMESAN SPAGHETTI SQUASH
MAKES 2 SERVINGS

1 medium spaghetti squash (2 to 2½ pounds)

1 cup water

2 tablespoons extra virgin olive oil

1 clove garlic, minced

¼ teaspoon salt

¼ teaspoon red pepper flakes

⅛ teaspoon black pepper

½ cup shredded Parmesan cheese

⅓ cup chopped fresh parsley

1 Cut squash in half; remove and discard seeds. Pour water into Instant Pot; place rack in pot. Place squash halves on rack, cut sides up.

2 Secure lid and move pressure release valve to Sealing position. Press Pressure Cook or Manual; cook at high pressure 7 minutes.

3 When cooking is complete, use quick release. Remove squash to plate; let stand until cool enough to handle. Use fork to shred squash into long strands, reserving shells for serving, if desired.

4 Pour out cooking water and dry pot with paper towel. Press Sauté; adjust heat to low. Add oil, garlic, salt, red pepper flakes and black pepper to pot; cook and stir 2 to 3 minutes or until garlic begins to turn golden. Turn off heat. Add squash, cheese and parsley; stir gently just until blended. Serve immediately.

LEMON–MINT RED POTATOES
MAKES 4 SERVINGS

- **2 pounds new red potatoes (1½ to 2 inches)**
- **⅓ cup water**
- **4 tablespoons chopped fresh mint, divided**
- **1 tablespoon olive oil**
- **1 teaspoon salt**
- **1 teaspoon grated lemon peel**
- **¾ teaspoon Greek seasoning or dried oregano**
- **¼ teaspoon black pepper**
- **1 tablespoon lemon juice**
- **1 tablespoon butter**

1 Combine potatoes, water, 2 tablespoons mint, oil, salt, lemon peel, Greek seasoning and pepper in Instant Pot; mix well.

2 Secure lid and move pressure release valve to Sealing position. Press Pressure Cook or Manual; cook at high pressure 6 minutes.

3 When cooking is complete, use quick release.

4 Press Sauté; add remaining 2 tablespoons mint, lemon juice and butter to pot. Cook and stir 2 minutes or until butter is melted and potatoes are completely coated.

TIP

Potatoes can stand at room temperature, covered, for up to 2 hours.

BEET AND ARUGULA SALAD
MAKES 6 SERVINGS

1 **cup water**

8 **medium beets (5 to 6 ounces each)**

⅓ **cup red wine vinegar**

¾ **teaspoon salt**

½ **teaspoon black pepper**

3 **tablespoons extra virgin olive oil**

1 **package (5 ounces) baby arugula**

1 **package (4 ounces) goat cheese with garlic and herbs, crumbled**

1 Pour water into Instant Pot; place rack in pot. Arrange beets on rack (or use steamer basket to hold beets).

2 Secure lid and move pressure release valve to Sealing position. Press Pressure Cook or Manual; cook at high pressure 20 minutes.

3 When cooking is complete, use natural release for 10 minutes, then release remaining pressure. Let beets stand until cool enough to handle.

4 Meanwhile, whisk vinegar, salt and pepper in large bowl. Slowly add oil in thin, steady stream, whisking until well blended. Remove 3 tablespoons dressing to medium bowl.

5 Peel beets and cut into wedges. Add warm beets to large bowl; toss to coat with dressing. Add arugula to medium bowl; toss gently to coat with dressing. Place arugula on platter or plates, top with beets and cheese.

RUSTIC GARLIC MASHED POTATOES
MAKES 6 SERVINGS

2 pounds baking potatoes, scrubbed and cut into 1-inch pieces

1 cup water

1¼ teaspoons salt, divided

1 teaspoon garlic powder

2 tablespoons butter, cut into small pieces

¼ teaspoon black pepper

¾ cup milk

1 Combine potatoes, water, 1 teaspoon salt and garlic powder in Instant Pot; mix well.

2 Secure lid and move pressure release valve to Sealing position. Press Pressure Cook or Manual; cook at high pressure 8 minutes.

3 When cooking is complete, use quick release. Stir in butter, remaining ¼ teaspoon salt and pepper. Gradually add milk, mashing with potato masher until deslred consistency is reached.

SPICED SWEET POTATOES
MAKES 4 TO 6 SERVINGS

2½ pounds sweet potatoes, peeled and cut into ½-inch pieces

½ cup water

2 tablespoons dark brown sugar

1 teaspoon salt

1 teaspoon ground cinnamon

½ teaspoon ground nutmeg

2 tablespoons butter, cut into small pieces

½ teaspoon vanilla

1 Combine sweet potatoes, water, brown sugar, salt, cinnamon and nutmeg in Instant Pot; mix well.

2 Secure lid and move pressure release valve to Sealing position. Press Pressure Cook or Manual; cook at high pressure 3 minutes.

3 When cooking is complete, use quick release.

4 Press Sauté; add butter and vanilla to pot. Cook 1 to 2 minutes or until butter is melted, stirring gently to blend.

RUSTIC GARLIC MASHED POTATOES

BUTTERNUT SQUASH WITH APPLES, CRANBERRIES AND WALNUTS

MAKES 4 SERVINGS

1 tablespoon butter

1 medium Granny Smith apple, peeled and cut into ½-inch pieces

3 cups cubed peeled butternut squash (¾-inch pieces)

½ cup water

3 tablespoons dried cranberries

2 teaspoons packed brown sugar

½ teaspoon salt

¼ teaspoon ground cinnamon

⅛ teaspoon black pepper

2 tablespoons chopped walnuts

1 Press Sauté; melt butter in Instant Pot. Add apple; cook about 5 minutes or until tender, stirring occasionally. Remove to plate; set aside.

2 Add squash, water, cranberries, brown sugar, salt, cinnamon and pepper to pot; stir until brown sugar is dissolved.

3 Secure lid and move pressure release valve to Sealing position. Press Pressure Cook or Manual; cook at high pressure 1 minute.

4 When cooking is complete, use quick release.

5 Press Sauté; add cooked apple to pot. Cook 2 minutes or until heated through, stirring occasionally. Gently stir in walnuts.

FAVORITE GREEN BEANS
MAKES 4 SERVINGS

1 cup water

1 pound fresh green beans, trimmed

2 tablespoons butter

1 teaspoon garlic salt

⅓ cup grated Parmesan cheese

1 Pour water into Instant Pot. Place rack in pot; place beans on rack. (Arrange beans perpendicular to rack to prevent beans from falling through. Or use steamer basket.)

2 Secure lid and move pressure release valve to Sealing position. Press Pressure Cook or Manual; cook at high pressure 2 minutes.

3 When cooking is complete, use quick release.

4 Remove rack from pot; drain off and discard cooking liquid. Return beans to pot; add butter and garlic salt. Press Sauté; cook and stir 1 minute or until butter is melted and beans are coated. Stir in cheese.

BLUE CHEESE POTATOES
MAKES 5 SERVINGS

2 pounds new red potatoes, peeled and cut into ¾-inch pieces

1¼ cups chopped green onions, divided

1 cup water

2 tablespoons olive oil, divided

1 teaspoon dried basil

1 teaspoon salt

¼ teaspoon black pepper

⅓ cup crumbled blue cheese

1 Combine potatoes, 1 cup green onions, water, 1 tablespoon oil, basil, salt and pepper in Instant Pot; mix well.

2 Secure lid and move pressure release valve to Sealing position. Press Pressure Cook or Manual; cook at high pressure 2 minutes.

3 When cooking is complete, use quick release.

4 Drain excess liquid from pot. Gently stir in cheese and remaining 1 tablespoon oil; season with additional salt and pepper. Top with remaining ¼ cup green onions.

FAVORITE GREEN BEANS

CAULIFLOWER AND POTATO MASALA
MAKES 6 SERVINGS

1 tablespoon olive or
   vegetable oil

2 teaspoons minced garlic

1 teaspoon minced
   fresh ginger

1 teaspoon salt

1 teaspoon cumin seeds
   or ½ teaspoon ground
   cumin

1 teaspoon ground
   coriander

1 teaspoon garam masala

1 can (about 14 ounces)
   diced tomatoes

1 head cauliflower (about
   1¼ pounds), broken
   into florets

1 pound red potatoes
   (2 large), peeled and
   cut into ½-inch wedges

2 tablespoons chopped
   fresh cilantro

1 Press Sauté; heat oil in Instant Pot. Add garlic,
   ginger, salt, cumin seeds, coriander and garam
   masala; cook and stir about 30 seconds or until
   fragrant. Add tomatoes; cook and stir 1 minute.
   Add cauliflower and potatoes; mix well.

2 Secure lid and move pressure release valve
   to Sealing position. Press Pressure Cook or
   Manual; cook at high pressure 2 minutes.

3 When cooking is complete, use quick release.
   Sprinkle with cilantro.

ORANGE-SPICED GLAZED CARROTS
MAKES 6 SERVINGS

1 package (32 ounces)
    baby carrots

½ cup orange juice

⅓ cup packed brown sugar

3 tablespoons butter,
    cut into small pieces

¾ teaspoon ground
    cinnamon

½ teaspoon salt

¼ teaspoon ground nutmeg

¼ cup water

2 tablespoons cornstarch

Grated orange peel
    (optional)

Chopped fresh parsley
    (optional)

1 Combine carrots, orange juice, brown sugar, butter, cinnamon, salt and nutmeg in Instant Pot; mix well.

2 Secure lid and move pressure release valve to Sealing position. Press Pressure Cook or Manual; cook at high pressure 2 minutes.

3 When cooking is complete, use quick release.

4 Stir water into cornstarch in small bowl until smooth. Press Sauté; add cornstarch mixture to pot. Cook and stir 1 to 2 minutes or until sauce thickens. Garnish with orange peel and parsley.

PARMESAN POTATO WEDGES
MAKES 4 TO 6 SERVINGS

2 pounds unpeeled red potatoes (about 6 medium), cut into ½-inch wedges

½ cup water

¼ cup finely chopped onion

2 tablespoons butter, cut into small pieces

1¼ teaspoons salt

1 teaspoon dried oregano

¼ teaspoon black pepper

¼ cup grated Parmesan cheese

1 Combine potatoes, water, onion, butter, salt, oregano and pepper in Instant Pot; mix well.

2 Secure lid and move pressure release valve to Sealing position. Press Pressure Cook or Manual; cook at high pressure 3 minutes.

3 When cooking is complete, use quick release. Stir in cheese.

SWEET AND SOUR CABBAGE
MAKES 4 SERVINGS

1½ pounds green or red cabbage or a combination, coarsely chopped

2 medium sweet apples (such as Fuji, Honeycrisp or Pink Lady), cut into ½-inch pieces

¼ cup water

3 tablespoons cider vinegar

3 tablespoons packed brown sugar

2 tablespoons olive oil

1 teaspoon salt

½ teaspoon caraway seeds

1 Combine cabbage, apples, water, vinegar, brown sugar, oil, salt and caraway seeds in Instant Pot; mix well.

2 Secure lid and move pressure release valve to Sealing position. Press Pressure Cook or Manual; cook at high pressure 3 minutes.*

3 When cooking is complete, use quick release. If there is excess liquid in pot, press Sauté and cook 3 to 4 minutes or until liquid has evaporated, stirring frequently.

A cook time of 3 minutes will result in crisp-tender cabbage. For softer cabbage, cook 4 minutes under pressure.

PARMESAN POTATO WEDGES

INSTANT COLLARD GREENS
MAKES 4 TO 6 SERVINGS

4 slices thick-cut bacon, cut into ½-inch pieces

1 pound collard greens, stems trimmed, roughly chopped

½ cup water or chicken broth

1 tablespoon cider vinegar

1 tablespoon packed brown sugar

¼ teaspoon salt

¼ teaspoon black pepper

¼ teaspoon red pepper flakes

1 Press Sauté; cook bacon in Instant Pot until crisp. Add half of greens; cook 1 minute or until greens begin to wilt, scraping up browned bits from bottom of pot. Add remaining greens; cook and stir 1 minute. Stir in water, vinegar, brown sugar, salt, black pepper and red pepper flakes; mix well.

2 Secure lid and move pressure release valve to Sealing position. Press Pressure Cook or Manual; cook at high pressure 20 minutes.

3 When cooking is complete, use quick release. Stir greens; serve warm.

CHUNKY RANCH POTATOES
MAKES 8 SERVINGS

3 pounds unpeeled red potatoes, quartered

½ cup water

1 teaspoon salt

½ cup ranch dressing

½ cup grated Parmesan cheese

¼ cup minced fresh chives

1 Combine potatoes, water and salt in Instant Pot; mix well.

2 Secure lid and move pressure release valve to Sealing position. Press Pressure Cook or Manual; cook at high pressure 5 minutes.

3 When cooking is complete, use quick release.

4 Add ranch dressing, cheese and chives to pot; stir gently to coat, breaking potatoes into smaller chunks.

INSTANT COLLARD GREENS

MASHED SWEET POTATOES AND PARSNIPS
MAKES 6 SERVINGS

2 large sweet potatoes (about 1½ pounds), peeled and cut into 1-inch pieces

2 medium parsnips (about 12 ounces), peeled and cut into ½-inch slices

½ cup water

1 teaspoon salt

¼ cup evaporated milk

2 tablespoons butter

⅛ teaspoon ground nutmeg

¼ cup chopped fresh chives or green onions

1 Combine sweet potatoes, parsnips, water and salt in Instant Pot; mix well.

2 Secure lid and move pressure release valve to Sealing position. Press Pressure Cook or Manual; cook at high pressure 10 minutes.

3 When cooking is complete, use quick release.

4 Add milk, butter and nutmeg to pot; mash with potato masher until smooth. Stir in chives.

BALSAMIC GREEN BEANS WITH ALMONDS
MAKES 4 SERVINGS

- 1 cup water
- 1 pound fresh green beans, trimmed
- 1 tablespoon extra virgin olive oil
- 2 teaspoons balsamic vinegar
- ½ teaspoon salt
- ¼ teaspoon black pepper
- 2 tablespoons sliced almonds, toasted*

To toast almonds, cook in small skillet over medium heat 1 to 2 minutes or until lightly browned, stirring frequently.

1 Pour water into Instant Pot. Place rack in pot; place beans on rack. (Arrange beans perpendicular to rack to prevent beans from falling through. Or use steamer basket.)

2 Secure lid and move pressure release valve to Sealing position. Press Pressure Cook or Manual; cook at high pressure 2 minutes.

3 When cooking is complete, use quick release. Remove rack from pot; place beans in large bowl.

4 Add oil, vinegar, salt and pepper; toss to coat. Sprinkle with almonds just before serving.

SIMPLE SQUASH AND CARROTS
MAKES 4 TO 6 SERVINGS

- 1½ tablespoons olive oil, divided
- 2 medium onions, coarsely chopped
- 2 pounds butternut squash, peeled and cut into 1-inch pieces (about 4 cups)
- 3 medium carrots, cut diagonally into ½-inch slices
- 1 teaspoon salt, divided
- ¼ teaspoon black pepper
- ½ cup water

1 Press Sauté; heat 1 tablespoon oil in Instant Pot. Add onions; cook and stir 2 minutes or until onions begin to soften. Add squash, carrots, ¾ teaspoon salt and pepper; mix well. Pour in water.

2 Secure lid and move pressure release valve to Sealing position. Press Pressure Cook or Manual; cook at high pressure 1 minute.

3 When cooking is complete, use quick release.

4 Drain excess liquid from pot. Add remaining ½ tablespoon oil and ¼ teaspoon salt; stir gently to coat.

BALSAMIC GREEN BEANS WITH ALMONDS

MEDITERRANEAN RED POTATOES
MAKES 4 SERVINGS

2 pounds unpeeled red potatoes, cut into 1-inch pieces

1 cup frozen pearl onions *or* 1 large onion, cut into 1-inch pieces

1 cup water

2 tablespoons olive oil, divided

1 teaspoon salt

1 teaspoon Italian seasoning

½ teaspoon garlic powder

¼ teaspoon black pepper

1 small tomato, seeded and chopped

½ cup crumbled feta cheese

2 tablespoons chopped black olives

1 Combine potatoes, onions, water, 1 tablespoon oil, salt, Italian seasoning, garlic powder and pepper in Instant Pot; mix well.

2 Secure lid and move pressure release valve to Sealing position. Press Pressure Cook or Manual; cook at high pressure 3 minutes.

3 When cooking is complete, use quick release.

4 Drain excess liquid from pot. Add remaining 1 tablespoon oil, tomato, cheese and olives; stir gently to blend.

Instant Pot

WINTER SQUASH RISOTTO
MAKES 4 TO 6 SERVINGS

2 tablespoons butter

1 tablespoon olive oil

1 large shallot or small onion, finely chopped

1½ cups uncooked arborio rice

1 teaspoon salt

½ teaspoon dried thyme

¼ teaspoon black pepper

¼ cup dry white wine

4 cups vegetable or chicken broth

2 cups cubed peeled butternut squash (½-inch pieces)

½ cup grated Parmesan or Romano cheese, plus additional for garnish

1 Press Sauté; heat butter and oil in Insant Pot. Add shallot; cook and stir 2 minutes or until softened. Add rice; cook and stir 4 minutes or until rice is translucent. Stir in salt, thyme and pepper.

2 Add wine; cook and stir about 1 minute or until evaporated. Stir in broth and squash; mix well.

3 Secure lid and move pressure release valve to Sealing position. Press Pressure Cook or Manual; cook at high pressure 6 minutes.

4 When cooking is complete, use quick release.

5 Press Sauté; adjust heat to low. Cook about 3 minutes or until risotto reaches desired consistency, stirring constantly. Stir in ½ cup cheese. Serve immediately with additional cheese.

BARLEY WITH ASPARAGUS AND PEAS
MAKES 6 SERVINGS

- 2 tablespoons olive oil, divided
- 1 pound asparagus, cut diagonally into 1½-inch pieces
- 2 shallots *or* 1 small onion, finely chopped, divided
- 1 clove garlic, minced
- 1½ cups uncooked pearl barley
- 2 cups vegetable broth
- Grated peel and juice of 1 lemon, divided
- 1 teaspoon salt
- ¼ teaspoon black pepper
- 1 cup thawed frozen peas
- ½ cup shredded Parmesan cheese, divided
- 2 green onions, cut into ¼-inch slices

1 Press Sauté; heat 1 tablespoon oil in Instant Pot. Add asparagus and 1 shallot; cook and stir 5 minutes or until asparagus is crisp-tender. Remove to small bowl.

2 Add remaining 1 tablespoon oil, 1 shallot and garlic to pot; cook and stir 1 minute. Add barley; cook and stir 2 minutes. Stir in broth, lemon peel, half of lemon juice, salt and pepper; mix well.

3 Secure lid and move pressure release valve to Sealing position. Press Pressure Cook or Manual; cook at high pressure 21 minutes.

4 When cooking is complete, use natural release for 10 minutes, then release remaining pressure.

5 Press Sauté; stir in asparagus, peas, half of cheese, remaining lemon juice and green onions. Cook 2 minutes or until heated through, stirring occasionally. Serve with remaining cheese.

GREEK RICE
MAKES 6 TO 8 SERVINGS

2 tablespoons butter

1¾ cups uncooked long grain rice, rinsed well and drained

1¾ cups vegetable or chicken broth

1 teaspoon Greek seasoning

1 teaspoon dried oregano

¼ teaspoon salt

1 cup pitted Kalamata olives, drained and chopped

¾ cup chopped roasted red peppers

Crumbled feta cheese (optional)

Chopped fresh Italian parsley (optional)

1 Press Sauté; melt butter in Instant Pot. Add rice; cook 5 to 6 minutes or until golden brown, stirring occasionally. Stir in broth, Greek seasoning, oregano and salt; mix well.

2 Secure lid and move pressure release valve to Sealing position. Press Pressure Cook or Manual; cook at high pressure 4 minutes.

3 When cooking is complete, use natural release for 10 minutes, then release remaining pressure.

4 Stir in olives and roasted peppers; garnish with cheese and parsley.

FARRO WITH BUTTERNUT SQUASH AND KALE
MAKES 6 TO 8 SERVINGS

2 tablespoons olive oil

1 small red onion, chopped

2 cloves garlic, minced

½ teaspoon dried thyme

1½ cups uncooked farro, rinsed and drained

2 cups vegetable broth

1½ teaspoons salt

¼ teaspoon black pepper

1 small butternut squash (about 1½ pounds), peeled and cut into ¾-inch pieces (3 cups)

1 small bunch lacinato kale, stemmed and cut crosswise into 1-inch-wide strips (3 cups)

½ cup grated Parmesan cheese

1 Press Sauté; heat oil in Instant Pot. Add onion; cook and stir 3 minutes or until softened. Add garlic and thyme; cook and stir 1 minute. Add farro; cook and stir 2 minutes. Stir in broth, salt and pepper; mix well.

2 Secure lid and move pressure release valve to Sealing position. Press Pressure Cook or Manual; cook at high pressure 7 minutes.

3 When cooking is complete, use quick release. Stir in squash and kale. Secure lid and move pressure release valve to Sealing position. Press Pressure Cook or Manual; cook at high pressure 3 minutes.

4 When cooking is complete, use natural release for 5 minutes, then release remaining pressure. Stir in cheese.

PEASANT RISOTTO
MAKES 4 SERVINGS

2 tablespoons olive oil, divided

3 ounces chopped prosciutto or ham

¼ cup chopped green onions

2 cloves garlic, minced

½ teaspoon dried sage

1 cup uncooked arborio rice

2¾ cups chicken broth

1 can (about 15 ounces) Great Northern beans, rinsed and drained

¼ teaspoon salt

1½ cups packed stemmed shredded Swiss chard

½ cup grated Parmesan cheese

1 Press Sauté; heat 1 tablespoon oil in Instant Pot. Add prosciutto; cook and stir 3 minutes. Add green onions, garlic and sage; cook and stir 1 minute. Add remaining 1 tablespoon oil and rice; cook and stir 2 minutes or until rice is translucent. Stir in broth, beans and salt; mix well.

2 Secure lid and move pressure release valve to Sealing position. Press Pressure Cook or Manual; cook at high pressure 6 minutes.

3 When cooking is complete, use quick release.

4 Press Sauté; add Swiss chard to pot. Cook 3 minutes or until chard is wilted, stirring constantly. Stir in cheese. Serve immediately.

BULGUR PILAF WITH CARAMELIZED ONIONS AND KALE

MAKES 4 SERVINGS

1 tablespoon olive oil

1 medium onion, cut into thin wedges

1 clove garlic, minced

2 cups chopped kale

2¾ cups vegetable or chicken broth

1 cup medium grain bulgur

1 teaspoon salt

¼ teaspoon black pepper

1 Press Sauté; heat oil in Instant Pot. Add onion; cook about 10 minutes or until golden brown, stirring frequently. Add garlic; cook and stir 1 minute. Add kale; cook and stir about 1 minute or until wilted. Stir in broth, bulgur, salt and pepper; mix well.

2 Secure lid and move pressure release valve to Sealing position. Press Pressure Cook or Manual; cook at high pressure 8 minutes.

3 When cooking is complete, use natural release for 5 minutes, then release remaining pressure.

BACON CHEDDAR GRITS

MAKES 4 SERVINGS

6 slices bacon, chopped

1 large shallot or small onion, finely chopped

1 serrano or jalapeño pepper, minced

3½ cups chicken broth

1 cup uncooked grits*

½ teaspoon salt

¼ teaspoon black pepper

1 cup (4 ounces) shredded Cheddar cheese

½ cup half-and-half

2 tablespoons finely chopped green onion

Do not use instant grits.

1 Press Sauté; cook bacon in Instant Pot until crisp. Drain on paper towel-lined plate. Drain off all but 1 tablespoon drippings.

2 Add shallot and serrano pepper to pot; cook and stir 2 minutes or until shallot is lightly browned. Add broth, grits, salt and black pepper; cook and stir 1 minute.

3 Secure lid and move pressure release valve to Sealing position. Press Pressure Cook or Manual; cook at high pressure 14 minutes.

4 When cooking is complete, use natural release for 10 minutes, then release remaining pressure. Stir grits until smooth. Add cheese, half-and-half and bacon; stir until well blended. Sprinkle with green onion.

MUSHROOM RISOTTO
MAKES 4 SERVINGS

2 tablespoons olive oil

¾ cup chopped shallots *or*
  1 small onion, chopped

8 ounces sliced mushrooms

3 cloves garlic, minced

1½ cups uncooked
  arborio rice

¼ cup Madeira wine

3½ cups vegetable broth

½ teaspoon salt

¼ teaspoon black pepper

⅔ cup grated Romano
  cheese

3 tablespoons chopped
  fresh parsley

2 tablespoons butter

1 Press Sauté; heat oil in Instant Pot. Add shallots; cook and stir 2 minutes or until softened. Add mushrooms; cook and stir about 6 minutes or until liquid evaporates and mushrooms begin to brown.

2 Add garlic; cook and stir 30 seconds. Add rice; cook and stir 1 minute. Add Madeira; cook and stir 1 minute or until almost evaporated. Stir in broth, salt and pepper; mix well.

3 Secure lid and move pressure release valve to Sealing position. Press Pressure Cook or Manual; cook at high pressure 6 minutes.

4 When cooking is complete, use quick release.

5 Press Sauté; adjust heat to low. Cook about 3 minutes or until risotto reaches desired consistency, stirring constantly. Stir in cheese, parsley and butter until blended.

CHEESY POLENTA
MAKES 6 SERVINGS

5 cups vegetable or
   chicken broth

½ teaspoon salt

1½ cups uncooked
   instant polenta

½ cup grated Parmesan
   cheese

¼ cup (½ stick) butter,
   cubed, plus additional
   for serving

   Fried sage leaves
   (optional)

1 Combine broth and salt in Instant Pot; slowly whisk in polenta until blended.

2 Secure lid and move pressure release valve to Sealing position. Press Pressure Cook or Manual; cook at high pressure 5 minutes.

3 When cooking is complete, use natural release for 5 minutes, then release remaining pressure.

4 Whisk in cheese and ¼ cup butter until well blended. (Polenta may appear separated immediately after cooking but will come together when stirred.) Serve with additional butter; garnish with sage.

TIP

Spread any leftover polenta in a baking dish and refrigerate until cold. Cut the cold polenta into sticks or slices, brush with olive oil and pan-fry or grill until lightly browned.

NOTE

Water may be subsituted for the broth; add an additional ½ teaspoon salt when whisking in the polenta.

SPANISH RICE
MAKES 6 TO 8 SERVINGS

1 tablespoon olive oil

1 small onion, chopped

2 cloves garlic, minced

2 cups uncooked brown rice, rinsed well and drained

1 can (about 14 ounces) diced tomatoes with green chiles

1 cup plus 2 tablespoons chicken broth or water

1 teaspoon salt

1 Press Sauté; heat oil in Instant Pot. Add onion and garlic; cook and stir 2 minutes. Add rice; cook and stir 2 minutes. Stir in tomatoes, broth and salt; mix well.

2 Secure lid and move pressure release valve to Sealing position. Press Pressure Cook or Manual; cook at high pressure 24 minutes.

3 When cooking is complete, use natural release for 10 minutes, then release remaining pressure. Fluff rice with fork.

EASY DIRTY RICE
MAKES 4 TO 6 SERVINGS

8 ounces uncooked bulk Italian sausage

1½ cups uncooked long grain rice, rinsed well and drained

1½ cups water

1 onion, finely chopped

1 green bell pepper, finely chopped

½ cup finely chopped celery

1½ teaspoons salt

¼ teaspoon black pepper

¼ teaspoon ground red pepper

½ cup chopped fresh parsley

1 Press Sauté; cook sausage in Instant Pot 6 to 8 minutes or until browned, stirring to break up meat. Drain fat.

2 Stir in rice, water, onion, bell pepper, celery, salt, black pepper and red pepper; mix well.

3 Secure lid and move pressure release valve to Sealing position. Press Pressure Cook or Manual; cook at high pressure 4 minutes.

4 When cooking is complete, use natural release for 10 minutes, then release remaining pressure. Stir in parsley.

BARLEY WITH CURRANTS AND PINE NUTS
MAKES 4 TO 6 SERVINGS

2 tablespoons butter

1 onion, finely chopped

2 cups vegetable broth

1 cup uncooked pearl barley

½ cup currants

½ teaspoon salt

¼ teaspoon black pepper

½ cup pine nuts, toasted*

*To toast pine nuts, cook in small skillet over medium heat 3 minutes or until lightly browned, stirring frequently.

1 Press Sauté; melt butter in Instant Pot. Add onion; cook and stir 5 minutes or until tender. Stir in broth, barley, currants, salt and pepper; mix well.

2 Secure lid and move pressure release valve to Sealing position. Press Pressure Cook or Manual; cook at high pressure 18 minutes.

3 When cooking is complete, use natural release for 10 minutes, then release remaining pressure.

4 Stir in pine nuts. Serve warm or at room temperature.

WHITE BEANS AND TOMATOES
MAKES 8 TO 10 SERVINGS

1 pound dried cannellini
   beans, soaked 8 hours
   or overnight

2 tablespoons olive oil

2 medium onions, chopped

1 tablespoon minced garlic

1 tablespoon tomato paste

2 teaspoons dried oregano

2 teaspoons salt

1 can (28 ounces)
   crushed tomatoes

2 cups water

   Black pepper (optional)

1 Drain and rinse beans. Press Sauté; heat oil in Instant Pot. Add onions; cook and stir 5 to 7 minutes or until tender and lightly browned.

2 Add garlic, tomato paste, oregano and salt; cook and stir 1 minute. Stir in beans, tomatoes and water; mix well.

3 Secure lid and move pressure release valve to Sealing position. Press Pressure Cook or Manual; cook at high pressure 16 minutes.

4 When cooking is complete, use natural release for 10 minutes, then release remaining pressure. Season with black pepper, if desired.

BLACK BEANS AND RICE
MAKES 6 TO 8 SERVINGS

1 tablespoon vegetable oil

1 onion, chopped

1 cup uncooked long grain rice, rinsed well and drained

¾ cup plus 2 tablespoons water

¾ cup chunky salsa, divided

4 teaspoons taco seasoning mix, divided

½ teaspoon salt

1 can (about 15 ounces) black beans, rinsed and drained

1 Press Sauté; heat oil in Instant Pot. Add onion; cook and stir 3 minutes or until softened. Add rice, water, ¼ cup salsa, 1 teaspoon taco seasoning and salt; mix well.

2 Secure lid and move pressure release valve to Sealing position. Press Pressure Cook or Manual; cook at high pressure 5 minutes.

3 When cooking is complete, use natural release for 10 minutes, then release remaining pressure. Stir rice.

4 Press Sauté; adjust heat to low. Add beans, remaining ½ cup salsa and 1 tablespoon taco seasoning; cook and stir about 3 minutes or until heated through.

FARRO RISOTTO WITH MUSHROOMS AND SPINACH

MAKES 4 SERVINGS

2 tablespoons olive oil, divided

1 onion, chopped

12 ounces cremini mushrooms, trimmed and quartered

1 teaspoon salt

¼ teaspoon black pepper

2 cloves garlic, minced

1 cup uncooked pearled farro

1 sprig fresh thyme

1½ cups vegetable broth

1 package (5 to 6 ounces) baby spinach

½ cup grated Parmesan cheese

1 Press Sauté; heat 1 tablespoon oil in Instant Pot. Add onion; cook and stir 5 minutes or until translucent. Add remaining 1 tablespoon oil, mushrooms, salt and pepper; cook about 8 minutes or until liquid evaporates and mushrooms are browned, stirring occasionally. Add garlic; cook and stir 1 minute. Add farro and thyme; cook and stir 1 minute. Stir in broth; mix well.

2 Secure lid and move pressure release valve to Sealing position. Press Pressure Cook or Manual; cook at high pressure 10 minutes.

3 When cooking is complete, use natural release for 10 minutes, then release remaining pressure. Remove and discard thyme sprig.

4 Add spinach and cheese; stir until spinach is wilted.

PRESSURE COOKING TIMES

Meat	MINUTES UNDER PRESSURE	PRESSURE	RELEASE
Beef, Bone-in Short Ribs	35 to 45	High	Natural
Beef, Brisket	60 to 75	High	Natural
Beef, Ground	8	High	Natural
Beef, Roast (round, rump or shoulder)	60 to 70	High	Natural
Beef, Stew Meat	20 to 25	High	Natural or Quick
Lamb, Chops	5 to 10	High	Quick
Lamb, Leg or Shanks	35 to 40	High	Natural
Lamb, Stew Meat	12 to 15	High	Quick
Pork, Baby Back Ribs	25 to 30	High	Natural
Pork, Chops	7 to 10	High	Quick
Pork, Ground	5	High	Quick
Pork, Loin	15 to 25	High	Natural
Pork, Shoulder or Butt	45 to 60	High	Natural
Pork, Stew Meat	15 to 20	High	Quick

Poultry	MINUTES UNDER PRESSURE	PRESSURE	RELEASE
Chicken Breasts, Bone-in	7 to 10	High	Quick
Chicken Breasts, Boneless	5 to 8	High	Quick
Chicken Thigh, Bone-in	10 to 14	High	Natural
Chicken Thigh, Boneless	8 to 10	High	Natural
Chicken Wings	10 to 12	High	Quick
Chicken, Whole	22 to 26	High	Natural
Eggs, Hard-Cooked (3 to 12)	9	Low	Quick

	MINUTES UNDER PRESSURE	PRESSURE	RELEASE
Turkey Breast, Bone-in	25 to 30	High	Natural
Turkey Breast, Boneless	15 to 20	High	Natural
Turkey Legs	35 to 40	High	Natural
Turkey, Ground	8 to 10	High	Quick

Seafood

	MINUTES UNDER PRESSURE	PRESSURE	RELEASE
Cod	2 to 3	Low	Quick
Crab	2 to 3	Low	Quick
Halibut	6	Low	Quick
Mussels	1 to 2	Low	Quick
Salmon	4 to 5	Low	Quick
Scallops	1	Low	Quick
Shrimp	2 to 3	Low	Quick
Swordfish	4 to 5	Low	Quick
Tilapia	3	Low	Quick

Dried Beans and Legumes

	UNSOAKED	SOAKED	PRESSURE	RELEASE
Black Beans	22 to 25	8 to 10	High	Natural
Black-Eyed Peas	9 to 11	3 to 5	High	Natural
Cannellini Beans	30 to 35	8 to 10	High	Natural
Chickpeas	35 to 40	18 to 22	High	Natural
Great Northern Beans	25 to 30	7 to 10	High	Natural

	UNSOAKED	SOAKED	PRESSURE	RELEASE
Kidney Beans	20 to 25	8 to 12	High	Natural
Lentils, Brown or Green	10 to 12	n/a	High	Natural
Lentils, Red or Yellow Split	1	n/a	High	Natural
Navy Beans	20 to 25	7 to 8	High	Natural
Pinto Beans	22 to 25	8 to 10	High	Natural
Split Peas	8 to 10	n/a	High	Natural

Grains

	LIQUID PER CUP	MINUTES UNDER PRESSURE	PRESSURE	RELEASE
Barley, Pearl	2	18 to 22	High	Natural
Barley, Whole	2½	30 to 35	High	Natural
Bulgur	3	8	High	Natural
Farro	2	10 to 12	High	Natural
Grits, Medium	4	12 to 15	High	10 minute natural
Millet	1½	1	High	Natural
Oats, Rolled	2	4 to 5	High	10 minute natural
Oats, Steel-Cut	3	10 to 13	High	10 minute natural
Quinoa	1½	1	High	10 minute natural
Polenta, Instant	3	5	High	5 minute natural
Rice, Arborio	2	6 to 7	High	Quick
Rice, Brown	1	22	High	10 minute natural
Rice, White Long Grain	1	4	High	10 minute natural

Vegetables

	MINUTES UNDER PRESSURE	PRESSURE	RELEASE
Artichokes, Whole	9 to 12	High	Natural
Beets, Medium Whole	18 to 24	High	Quick
Brussels Sprouts, Whole	2 to 3	High	Quick

	MINUTES UNDER PRESSURE	PRESSURE	RELEASE
Cabbage, Sliced	3 to 5	High	Quick
Carrots, Sliced	2 to 4	High	Quick
Cauliflower, Florets	2 to 3	High	Quick
Cauliflower, Whole	3 to 5	High	Quick
Corn on the Cob	2 to 4	High	Quick
Eggplant	3 to 4	High	Quick
Fennel, Sliced	3 to 4	High	Quick
Green Beans	2 to 4	High	Quick
Kale	3	High	Quick
Leeks	3	High	Quick
Okra	3	High	Quick
Potatoes, Baby or Fingerling	6 to 10	High	Natural
Potatoes, New	7 to 9	High	Natural
Potatoes, 1-inch pieces	4 to 6	High	Quick
Potatoes, Sweet, 1-inch pieces	3	High	Quick
Potatoes, Sweet, Whole	8 to 12	High	Natural
Spinach	1	High	Quick
Squash, Acorn, Halved	7	High	Natural
Squash, Butternut, 1-inch pieces	4 to 6	High	Quick
Squash, Spaghetti, Halved	6 to 10	High	Natural
Tomatoes, cut into pieces for sauce	5	High	Natural

METRIC CONVERSION CHART

VOLUME MEASUREMENTS (dry)

$\frac{1}{8}$ teaspoon = 0.5 mL
$\frac{1}{4}$ teaspoon = 1 mL
$\frac{1}{2}$ teaspoon = 2 mL
$\frac{3}{4}$ teaspoon = 4 mL
1 teaspoon = 5 mL
1 tablespoon = 15 mL
2 tablespoons = 30 mL
$\frac{1}{4}$ cup = 60 mL
$\frac{1}{3}$ cup = 75 mL
$\frac{1}{2}$ cup = 125 mL
$\frac{2}{3}$ cup = 150 mL
$\frac{3}{4}$ cup = 175 mL
1 cup = 250 mL
2 cups = 1 pint = 500 mL
3 cups = 750 mL
4 cups = 1 quart = 1 L

VOLUME MEASUREMENTS (fluid)

1 fluid ounce (2 tablespoons) = 30 mL
4 fluid ounces ($\frac{1}{2}$ cup) = 125 mL
8 fluid ounces (1 cup) = 250 mL
12 fluid ounces ($1\frac{1}{2}$ cups) = 375 mL
16 fluid ounces (2 cups) = 500 mL

WEIGHTS (mass)

$\frac{1}{2}$ ounce = 15 g
1 ounce = 30 g
3 ounces = 90 g
4 ounces = 120 g
8 ounces = 225 g
10 ounces = 285 g
12 ounces = 360 g
16 ounces = 1 pound = 450 g

DIMENSIONS

$\frac{1}{16}$ inch = 2 mm
$\frac{1}{8}$ inch = 3 mm
$\frac{1}{4}$ inch = 6 mm
$\frac{1}{2}$ inch = 1.5 cm
$\frac{3}{4}$ inch = 2 cm
1 inch = 2.5 cm

OVEN TEMPERATURES

250°F = 120°C
275°F = 140°C
300°F = 150°C
325°F = 160°C
350°F = 180°C
375°F = 190°C
400°F = 200°C
425°F = 220°C
450°F = 230°C

BAKING PAN SIZES

Utensil	Size in Inches/Quarts	Metric Volume	Size in Centimeters
Baking or Cake Pan (square or rectangular)	8×8×2	2 L	20×20×5
	9×9×2	2.5 L	23×23×5
	12×8×2	3 L	30×20×5
	13×9×2	3.5 L	33×23×5
Loaf Pan	8×4×3	1.5 L	20×10×7
	9×5×3	2 L	23×13×7
Round Layer Cake Pan	8×1½	1.2 L	20×4
	9×1½	1.5 L	23×4
Pie Plate	8×1¼	750 mL	20×3
	9×1¼	1 L	23×3
Baking Dish or Casserole	1 quart	1 L	—
	1½ quart	1.5 L	—
	2 quart	2 L	—